D1174171

Working With People

A Selected Social Casework
Bibliography

Compiled by MARION S. BLANK

**Revised and Enlarged
Second Edition**

Working With People

A Selected Social Casework
Bibliography

Compiled by MARION S. BLANK

Revised and Enlarged
Second Edition

FAMILY SERVICE ASSOCIATION OF AMERICA
NEW YORK

Copyright © 1982 by
Family Service Association of America
44 East 23rd Street, New York, New York 10010

Library of Congress Cataloging in Publication Data

Blank, Marion.
    Working with people.'

    1. Social case work—Bibliography.   I. Title.
Z7164.C4B6   1981 [HV43]   016.3613'2   81-43789
ISBN 0-87304-193-3   AACR2

Printed in the United States of America

TABLE OF CONTENTS

Preface to Second Edition

When Family Service Association of America indicated the usefulness of this bibliography to practitioners, educators, and students and requested that I prepare an updated second edition of *Working With People*, I willingly agreed to do so. Although the original edition was a combined effort of many people, in this edition all responsibility for changes and what is included rests solely with me.

I want to thank two people for their assistance with this edition—Kathryn Paternoster, a recent graduate of the Boston University School of Social Work, for her efforts in verifying and completing some references, and, particularly, Robin Chapman, the capable Casework Sequence secretary, for her competent typing job and her willingness to assume this additional task over and above her already busy schedule.

MARION S. BLANK
Professor
Boston University School of Social Work,
Boston, Massachusetts.

Summer 1981

Preface to First Edition

Social casework uses a systems approach. It is concerned with social problems, with the relationships between micro and macro systems, and with the impact of various systems on the individual and family and their impact on other systems. Although the focus of social casework is on the individual and family systems, both are constantly related to interactional systems in the community, including various support systems and resources.

The field of social casework relies heavily on input from ego psychology. It is the function of the ego to perceive, select, regulate, execute, and integrate the interaction between internal need and want and external demand and responsibility. The ego attempts to modify internal processes of thinking, feeling, and doing in relation to reality demands, or to modify objective reality in relation to subjective needs. The ego uses protective techniques to maintain equilibrium during the process of change.

Because the total field of social work is continually influenced by changing times and changing concepts about how best to meet a variety of social needs, some historical perspective on these changes is important for today's caseworker in understanding his activity as it is affected by the development of the casework method as a professional process.

Social casework is particularly concerned with helping with social functioning. This may be defined by the individual's capacity at any given time to fulfill his responsibilities and expectations of the social roles asssociated with his age, sex, and sociocultural circumstances. Social functioning underlines the social conditions of the individual and family. Social and environmental opportunities as well as the individual's and family's capacities, motivation, and adaptive mechanisms need be carefully considered. Through the medium of a relationship and the use of various interventions, social casework helps to solve, modify, and ameliorate problems in social functioning.

The social caseworker is a social worker who has a knowledge and appreciation of other modalities and the ways in which various modalities complement each other in serving people. The caseworker sees therapeutic intervention as effected not according to method but according to human need. He is cognizant of all methods in his deliberations, and he uses all methods on behalf of his clients through his own activity, through his collaboration with others, and through referral.

The caseworker's functions are over and above individual cases. He needs to be concerned when the needs of his clients are not met because of inadequate knowledge, skill, or resources, or a combination of these. Development of practice and services takes place through documentation to administration in individual cases, formal research to enlighten others as to practice, administrative action, and community and social action and advocacy. Throughout the process of casework, the social worker should be aware of these functions, should see them as part of his responsibility, and should act on them in avenues available to him—the agency, the profession, and citizen groups—to effect individual and institutional change.

Initially, this bibliography was prepared by the faculty of the Boston University School of Social Work Casework Sequence as a support to the classroom teaching of the Social Casework Sequence and to students' practice in their field work assignments. It became clear, however, that it was a reading resource that extended beyond the students' current program. The bibliography was referred to as "a forever bib," which underlined the importance of continuing to read as students become professional practitioners and to search for additional readings to strengthen knowledge. As alumni of the school and other social workers in the community expressed an interest in having the bibliography, it became apparent that it might have a usefulness far more widespread than the current student body and the Boston community. The present highly selected bibliography is a recent revision of the earlier work. New headings have been added, such as Women, Sexual Deviance, Other Sexual Orientations, and Feminist Therapy, to make the bibliography more relevant to the current practice scene.

The bibliography is structured in six major parts:

Basic Readings includes casework texts and readings on history and values. It provides a basic framework for what the student will later encounter in casework.

Essential Elements of Practice with the Individual and Family relates to the orderly process of study/exploration, diagnosis/assessment, treatment/intervention, and evaluation. This part stresses the significance of differential assessment and differential intervention. Included also are readings on the agency and community and on the key elements in the various stages of the casework process—beginning, engaging the client, contract, termination and transfer—with attention directed to the use of supervision and consultation and inter- and intra-agency collaboration.

The third section, *Special Populations,* covers such topics as age groupings, women, minorities, and particular problem areas, for example, alcoholism and other drug abuse, out-of-wedlock pregnancy and unwed parenthood, and retardation.

Evaluation is the final and important step of critical appraisal in the casework process. This section includes readings on general principles of evaluation and lists some research developments in casework practice.

The fifth section, *Additional Frames of Reference,* includes references on a variety of helping approaches, such as behavior modification and transactional analysis, which are sometimes used in conjunction with casework and sometimes in place of it.

The last part, *Some New Approaches and Issues in Casework Practice,** includes readings in a variety of areas such as accountability, advocacy, family life education, fees, paraprofessionals, private practice, and self-help groups.

The compilation of the bibliography was a combined effort by many people, including faculty who taught in the school's Social Casework Sequence, Mrs. Alma Berson, Mrs. Ruth Cowin, Miss Mary Louise Dillon, Mrs. Mildred Flashman, Dr. Sylvia Krakow, Miss Betty Milhendler, Miss Jeane Murphy (now deceased), Dr. Rose Segal, Mrs. Martha Williams, and students with particular interest and expertise in particular areas. Thanks are due to the many contributors to this production.

MARION S. BLANK
Professor
Chairperson of the Social Casework Sequence
Boston University School of Social Work,
Boston, Massachusetts.

Summer 1978

*Retitled in the Second Edition "Evolving Casework Practice: Approaches and Issues."

I. Basic Readings (Including History)

Bartlett, Harriett. *The Common Base of Social Work Practice*. New York: National Association of Social Workers, 1970.

Biestek, Felix, and Gehrig, Clyde. *Client Self-Determination in Social Work: A Fifty Year History*. Chicago: Loyola University Press, 1978.

Blanck, Gertrude. "Toward the Elaboration of Practice Theory." *Smith College Studies in Social Work* 47 (March 1977).

Blanck, Rubin. "The Case for Casework." *Smith College Studies in Social Work* 49 (June 1979).

_____."Practice Theory Then and Now." *Smith College Studies in Social Work* 47 (March 1977).

Bloom, Allan. "Social Work and the English Language." *Social Casework** 61 (June 1980).

Bloom, Martin. "Challenges to the Helping Professions and the Response of Scientific Practice." *Social Service Review* 52 (December 1978).

Briar, Scott, and Miller, Henry. *Problems and Issues in Social Casework*. New York: Columbia University Press, 1971.

Diner, Steven. "Scholarship in the Quest for Social Welfare—A Fifty-Year History of the Social Service Review." *Social Service Review* 51 (March 1977).

Epstein, Laura. *Helping People: The Task-Centered Approach*. St. Louis: C. V. Mosby, Co., 1980.

Ewalt, Patricia, ed. *Toward a Definition of Clinical Social Work*. Washington, D.C.: National Association of Social Workers, 1980.

Fischer, Joel. *Effective Casework Practice: An Eclectic Approach*. New York: McGraw-Hill, 1978.

Frank, Margaret, "Clinical Social Work: Past, Present and Future, Challenges and Dilemmas." *Smith College Studies in Social Work* 50 (June 1980).

Fraiberg, Selma. "Psychoanalysis and Social Work: A Reexamination of the Issues." *Smith College Studies in Social Work* 48 (March 1978).

Freed, Anne. "Social Casework: More than a Modality." *Social Casework* 58 (April 1977).

---

*Beginning with the January 1979 issue (vol. 60), the journal *Social Casework* was renamed *Social Casework: The Journal of Contemporary Social Work*.

Germain, Carel, and Hartman, Ann. "People and Ideas in the History of Social Work Practice." *Social Casework* 61 (June 1980).

Goldmeier, John. "The Legacy of Mary Richmond in Education and Practice." *Social Casework* 54 (May 1973).

Goldstein, Eda. "Knowledge Base of Clinical Social Work." *Social Work* 25 (May 1980).

Gottesfeld, Mary, and Pharis, Mary. *Profiles in Social Work*. New York: Behavioral Publications, 1976.

Hamilton, Gordon. *Theory and Practice of Social Casework*. 2d ed. New York: Columbia University Press, 1951.

Hardman, Dale. "Not With My Daughter You Don't." *Social Work* 20 (July 1975).

Hartman, Ann. "But What Is Social Casework?" *Social Casework* 52 (July 1971).

Hollis, Florence. "On Revisiting Social Work." *Social Casework*: 61 (January 1980).

_____, and Woods, Mary. *Casework: A Psychosocial Therapy*, 3d ed. (New York: Random House, 1972.

Howe, Michael, and Schuerman, John. "Trends in the Social Work Literature: 1957–72." *Social Service Review* 48 (June 1974).

Kassel, Suzanne, and Kane, Rosalie. "Self-Determination Dissected." *Clinical Social Work Journal* 8 (Fall 1980).

Katz, Sanford. *Creativity in Social Work: Selected Writings of Lydia Rapoport*. Philadelphia: Temple University Press, 1975.

Kendall, Katherine. "Signals from an Illustrious Past." *Social Casework* 58 (June 1977).

Leighninger, Leslie. "The Generalist—Specialist Debate in Social Work." *Social Service Review* 54 (March 1980).

Levy, Charles. "Personal Versus Professional Values: The Practitioner's Dilemmas." *Clinical Social Work Journal* 4 (Summer 1976).

_____. *Social Work Ethics*. New York: Human Sciences Press, 1980.

Meyer, Carol. "Purposes and Boundaries—Casework Fifty Years Later." *Social Casework* 54 (May 1973).

_____. "What Directions for Direct Practice?" *Social Work* 24 (July 1979)

Mishne, Judith, ed. *Psychotherapy and Training in Clinical Social Work*. New York: Halsted Press, 1980.

Moore-Kirkland, Janet, and Irey, Karen. "A Reappraisal of Confidentiality." *Social Work* 26 (July 1981).

Nelsen, Judith. *Communication Theory and Social Work Practice.* Chicago: University of Chicago Press, 1980.

Noble, Dorinda, and King, John. "Values: Passing on the Torch without Burning the Runner." *Social Casework* 62 (December 1981).

Orcutt, Ben, ed. *Poverty and Social Casework Services: Selected Papers.* Metuchen, N.J.: Scarecrow Press, 1974.

Parad, Howard, ed. *Crisis Intervention: Selected Readings.* New York: Family Service Association of America, 1965.

————, ed. *Ego Psychology and Dynamic Casework: Papers from the Smith College for Social Work.* New York: Family Service Association of America, 1958.

Parad, Howard, and Miller, Roger, eds. *Ego-Oriented Casework, Problems and Perspectives.* New York: Family Service Association of America, 1963.

Perlman, Helen. "Are We Creating Dependency?" *Social Service Review* 34 (September 1960). Also in Perlman's *Perspectives in Social Casework.*

————. "Believing and Doing: Values in Social Work Education." *Social Casework* 57 (June 1976).

————. "Can Casework Work?" *Social Service Review* 42 (December 1968). Also in Perlman's *Perspectives in Social Casework.*

————. *Persona: Social Role and Personality.* Chicago: University of Chicago Press, 1968.

————. *Perspectives in Social Casework.* Philadelphia: Temple University Press, 1971.

————. *Social Casework: A Problem Solving Process.* Chicago: University of Chicago Press, 1957.

————, ed. *Helping: Charlotte Towle on Social Work and Social Casework.* Chicago: University of Chicago Press, 1969.

Pumphrey, Muriel. "Lasting and Outmoded Concepts in the Caseworker's Heritage." *Social Casework* 54 (May 1973).

Rapoport, Lydia. "Social Casework: An Appraisal and An Affirmation." *Smith College Studies in Social Work* 39 (June 1969). Also in Katz's *Creativity in Social Work.*

Reamer, Frederic. "Ethical Content in Social Work." *Social Casework* 61 (November 1980).

Reid, William. *The Task-Centered System.* New York: Columbia University Press, 1978.

———, and Epstein, Laura, eds. *Task-Centered Casework.* New York: Columbia University Press, 1972.

———. *Task-Centered Practice.* New York: Columbia University Press, 1977.

———, and Shyne, Ann. *Brief and Extended Casework.* New York: Columbia University Press, 1969.

Reynolds, Bertha. *Social Work and Social Living.* 1951 reprint ed. Washington, D.C.: National Association of Social Workers, 1975.

———. *The Uncharted Journey.* New York: Citadel Press, 1963.

Richmond, Mary. *Social Diagnosis.* New York: Russell Sage Foundation, 1917.

———. *What is Social Casework?* New York: Russell Sage Foundation, 1922.

Roberts, Robert, and Nee, Robert, eds. *Theories of Social Casework.* Chicago: University of Chicago Press, 1970.

Siporin, Max. "Practice Theory for Clinical Social Work." *Clinical Social Work Journal* 7 (Spring 1979).

Strean, Herbert. *Clinical Social Work: Theory and Practice.* New York: The Free Press, 1978.

———. *Personality Theory and Social Work Practice.* Metuchen, N.J.: Scarecrow Press, 1975.

———, ed. *Social Casework: Theories in Action.* Metuchen, N.J.: Scarecrow Press, 1971.

Towle, Charlotte. *Common Human Needs.* New York: National Association of Social Workers, 1952, and 2d ed., 1965.

Truax, Charles, and Carkhuff, Robert. *Toward Effective Counseling and Psychotherapy.* Chicago: Aldine Publishing, 1967.

Turner, Francis, ed. *Differential Diagnosis and Treatment in Social Work.* New York: The Free Press, 1968, and 2d ed., 1976.

———. *Psychosocial Therapy: A Social Work Perspective.* New York: The Free Press, 1978.

———, ed. *Social Work Treatment: Interlocking Theoretical Approaches.* New York: The Free Press, 1974, and 2d ed., 1979.

Upham, Frances. *Ego Analysis in the Helping Professions.* New York: Family Service Association of America, 1973.

William, Henry; Sims, John; and Spray, Lee. *The Fifth Profession: Becoming a Psychotherapist.* San Francisco: Jossey-Bass, 1971.

II. Essential Elements of Practice with the Individual and Family

A. AGENCY AND COMMUNITY

Ambrosino Salvatore. "A Family Agency Reaches Out to a Slum Ghetto." *Social Work* 11 (October 1966).

Ayres, Alice. "Neighborhood Services: People Caring for People." *Social Casework* 54 (April 1973).

Bertsche, Anne, and Horejsi, Charles. "Coordination of Client Services." *Social Work* 25 (March 1980).

Cahn, Charles, Jr. "How to Assess Your Agency: A Primer for Board Members." *Child Welfare* 56 (May 1977).

Collins, Alice, and Pancoast, Diane. *Natural Helping Networks: A Strategy for Prevention*. Washington, D.C.: National Association of Social Workers, 1976.

Davies, Martin. "The Assessment of Environment in Social Work Research." *Social Casework* 55 (January 1974).

Finch, Wilbur. "Social Worker Versus Bureaucracy." *Social Work* 21 (September 1976).

Giordano, Peggy. "The Client's Perspective in Agency Evaluation." *Social Work* 22 (January 1977).

Grinnell, Richard, Jr., and Kyte, Nancy. "Modifying the Environment." *Social Work* 19 (July 1974).

Grosser, Charles. "Local Residents as Mediators Between Middle-Class Professional Workers and Lower-Class Clients." *Social Service Review* 40 (March 1966).

Hall, Julian; Smith, Kathleen; and Bradley, Anna. "Delivering Mental Health Services to the Urban Poor." *Social Work* 15 (April 1970).

Homer, Louise. "Community Based Resources for Runaway Girls." *Social Casework* 54 (October 1973).

Jones, Terry. "Institutional Racism in the U.S." *Social Work* 19 (March 1974).

McKelvy, Doris. "Agency Change: A Response to the Needs of Black Families and Children." *Child Welfare* 60 (March 1981).

Maluccio, Anthony. "The Influence of the Agency Environment on Clinical Practice." *Journal of Sociology and Social Welfare* 6 (November 1979).

Meyer, Carol. *Social Work Practice: The Changing Landscape.* New York: The Free Press, 1976. See Chap. 2, "The Way People Live: The Context of Social Work Practice."

Pawlak, Edward. "Organization Tinkering." *Social Work* 21 (September 1976).

Randolph, Jerry, and Taylor, James. "Short-changed in the Job Market: A Shopper's Guide." *Social Casework* 60 (December 1979).

Resnick, Herman. "Effecting Internal Change in Human Service Organizations." *Social Casework* 58 (November 1977).

Siporin, Max. *Introduction to Social Work Practice.* New York: Macmillan, 1975. See Appendix B, "Descriptive Reports on a Social Agency and on a Community."

B. RELATIONSHIP (INCLUDING TRANSFERENCE)

Appel, Gerald. "Some Aspects of Transference and Countertransference in Marital Counseling." *Social Casework* 47 (May 1966).

Barish, Samoan. "Lend Me Your Ear: An Explanation of Clinical Listening." *Clinical Social Work Journal* 3 (Summer 1975).

Biestek, Felix. *The Casework Relationship.* Chicago: Loyola University Press, 1957.

Bradmiller, Linde. "Self-disclosure in the Helping Relationship." *Social Work Research and Abstracts* 14 (Summer 1978).

Calnek, Maynard. "Racial Factors in Countertransference: The Black Therapist and the Black Client." *American Journal of Orthopsychiatry* 40 (January 1970).

Carpenter, Patricia. "A View of the Client-Worker Encounter." *Smith College Studies in Social Work* 47 (June 1977).

Edwards, Joyce. "The Therapist as a Catalyst in Separation—Individuation." *Clinical Social Work Journal* 4 (Fall 1976).

Epstein, Lawrence, and Feiner, Arthur. *Countertransference.* New York: Jason Aronson, 1979.

Feldman, Yonata. "Listening and Understanding." *Clinical Social Work Journal* 3 (Summer 1975).

Fuchs, Lester. "Reflections on Touching and Transference in Psychotherapy." *Clinical Social Work Journal* 3:3 (Fall 1975).

Gareffa, Domenic, and Neff, Stanley. "Management of the Client's Seductive Behavior." *Smith College Studies in Social Work* 44 (February 1974).

Garrett, Annette. "The Worker-Client Relationship." In *Ego Psychology and Dynamic Casework: Papers from the Smith College for Social Work*. Edited by Howard Parad. New York: Family Service Association of America, 1958.

Gottesfeld, Mary, and Lieberman, Florence. "The Pathological Therapist." *Social Casework* 60 (July 1979).

Gottlieb, Werner, and Stanley, Joseph. "Mutual Goals and Goal Setting in Casework." *Social Casework* 48 (October 1967).

Hamilton, Gordon. *Theory and Practice of Social Casework*. 2d rev. ed. New York: Columbia University Press, 1957. See especially Chap. 2, "The Use of Relationship."

Hollis, Florence. *Casework: A Psychosocial Therapy*. 2d ed. New York: Random House, 1972. See Chap. 13, "The Client-Worker Relationship."

Kadushin, Alfred. *The Social Work Interview*. New York: Columbia University Press, 1972. See especially Chap. 2, "Communication and Relationship."

Kaplan, Bert. "Overvaluing the Therapist: The Search for a Good Object." *Clinical Social Work Journal* 3 (Fall 1975).

Keefe, Thomas. "The Development of Empathic Skill: A Study." *Journal of Education for Social Work* 15 (Spring 1979).

_____. "Empathy: The Critical Skill." *Social Work* 21 (January 1976).

_____. "Empathy, Skill, and Critical Consciousness." *Social Casework* 61 (September 1980).

Kwawer, Jay. "Transference and Countertransference in Homosexuality—Changing Psychoanalytic Views." *American Journal of Psychotherapy* 34 (January 1980).

Lackie, Bruce. "Nonverbal Communication in Clinical Social Work Practice." *Clinical Social Work Journal* 5 (Spring 1977).

Lidz, Theodore. *The Person: His and Her Development Throughout the Life Cycle*. New York: Basic Books, 1976. See especially Chap. 21, "The Therapeutic Relationship."

Lieberman, Florence, and Gottesfeld, Mary. "The Repulsive Client." *Clinical Social Work Journal* 1 (Spring 1973).

Mayer, John, and Timms, Noel. "Clash in Perspective Between Worker and Client." *Social Casework* 50 (January 1969).

Mendes, Helen. "Countertransferences and Counter-Culture Clients." *Social Casework* 58 (March 1977).

Menninger, Karl. "Transference and Countertransference: The Involuntary Participation of Both Parties in the Treatment Situation." *Theory of Psychoanalytic Technique*. New York: Basic Books, 1958.

Miller, Donna. "The Influence of the Patient's Sex on Clinical Judgment." *Smith College Studies in Social Work* 44 (February 1974).

Nicholls, Grace. "The Science and Art of Casework Relationship." *Smith College Studies in Social Work* 36 (February 1966).

Palombo, Joseph. "Theories of Narcissism and the Practice of Social Work." *Clinical Social Work Journal* 4 (Fall 1976).

Perlman, Helen. *Relationship: The Heart of Helping People*. Chicago: University of Chicago Press, 1979.

Perman, Joshua. "Role of Transference in Casework with Public Assistance Families." *Social Work* 8 (October 1963).

Perry, Sylvia. "The Conscious Use of Relationship with the Neurotic Client." In Parad's *Ego Psychology and Dynamic Casework*. (See entry under Garrett above).

Reid, Kenneth. "Non-rational Dynamics of the Client-Worker Interaction." *Social Casework* 58 (December 1977).

Reid, William. "Client and Practitioner Variables Affecting Treatment." *Social Casework* 45 (December 1964).

Rhodes, Sonya. "The Personality of the Worker: An Unexplored Dimension in Treatment." *Social Casework* 60 (May 1979).

Rubin, Carol. "Notes From a Pregnant Therapist." *Social Work* 25 (May 1980).

Schwartz, Mary. "Helping the Worker with Countertransference." *Social Work* 23 (May 1978).

———. "Importance of the Sex of Worker and Client." *Social Work* 19 (March 1974).

Searles, Harold. *Countertransference and Related Subjects*. New York: International Universities Press, 1975

Smaldino, Angelo. "The Importance of Hope in the Casework Relationship." *Social Casework* 56 (June 1975).

Spiegel, John. "Some Cultural Aspects of Transference and Countertransference." In *Individual and Family Dynamics*. Edited by Jules Mosserman. New York: Grune and Stratton, 1959.

Stewart, James, Jr.; Lauderdale, Michael; and Shuttlesworth, Guy. "The Poor and the Motivation Fallacy." *Social Work* 17 (November 1972).

Studt, Elliot. "Worker-Client Authority Relationship in Social Work." *Social Work* 4 (January 1959).

Thale, Thomas. 'Effects of Medication on the Caseworker-Client Relationship." *Social Casework* 54 (January 1973).

Zentner, Ervin. "The Use of Letters to Sustain the Casework Process." *Social Casework* 48 (March 1967).

C. ENGAGING THE CLIENT (INCLUDING RESISTANCE)

Anderson, Gary. "Enhancing Listening Skills for Work with Abusing Parents." *Social Casework* 60 (December 1979).

Cowan, Barbara et al. "Holding Unwilling Clients in Treatment." *Social Casework* 50:3 (March 1969).

Dedmon, Rachel. "Mutuality Conceptualized for Direct Service." *Clinical Social Work Journal* 1 (Fall 1973).

Goldberg, Gale. "Breaking the Communication Barrier: The Initial Interview with an Abusing Parent." *Child Welfare* 54 (April 1975).

Gourse, Judith, and Chescheir, Martha. "Authority Issues in Treating Resistant Families." *Social Casework* 62 (February 1981).

Henry, Charlotte. "Motivation in Non-voluntary Clients." *Social Casework* 39 (February-March, 1958).

Hepworth, Dean. "Early Removal of Resistance in Task-Centered Casework." *Social Work* 24 (July 1979).

Leader, Arthur. "The Problem of Resistance in Social Work." *Social Work* 3 (April 1958).

Love, Sidney, and Mayer, Herta. "Going Along with Defenses in Resistive Families." *Social Casework* 40 (February 1959).

Mayo, Claire, and True, Susanne. "Turning Negatives into Positives in Treatment." *Social Casework* 48 (February 1967).

Molyneux, I.E. "Resistance in Casework Relationships." *Social Worker* 34 (November 1966).

Mullen, Edward. "Differences in Worker Style in Casework." *Social Casework* 50 (June 1969).

Murdach, Allison. "Bargaining and Persuasion with Nonvoluntary Clients." *Social Work* 25 (November 1980).

Nelsen, Judith. "Dealing with Resistance in Social Work Practice." *Social Casework* 56 (December 1975).

Oxley, Genevieve. "The Caseworker's Expectation and Client Motivation." *Social Casework* 47 (July 1966).

———. "Involuntary Clients' Responses to a Treatment Experience." *Social Casework* 58 (December 1977).

Perlman, Helen. "The Client's Treatability." *Social Work* 1 (October 1956).

Powell, Thomas. "Negative Expectations of Treatment: Some Ideas About the Source and Management of Two Types." *Clinical Social Work Journal* 1 (Fall 1973).

Strean, Herbert. "Helping Patients Fail." *Psychoanalytic Review* 60 (Fall 1973).

Swanson, Mary, and Woolson, Allen. "Psychotherapy with the Unmotivated Patient." *Psychotherapy: Theory, Research and Practice* 10 (Summer 1973).

Tomlinson, Rod, and Peters, Peg. "An Alternative to Placing Children: Intensive and Extensive Therapy with 'Disengaged' Families." *Child Welfare* 60 (February 1981).

Tropp, Emanual. "Three Problematic Concepts: Client, Help, Worker." *Social Casework* 55 (January 1974).

D. INTAKE

Banks, George et al. "The Effects of Counselor, Race and Training upon the Counseling Process with Negro Clients in Initial Interviews." *Journal of Clinical Psychology* 23 (January 1967).

Berliner, Arthur. "Fundamentals of Intake Interviewing." *Child Welfare* 56 (December 1977).

Blenkner, Mararet. "Predictive Factors in the Initial Interview in Family Casework." *Social Service Review* 28 (March 1954).

Duehn, Wayne, and Mayadas, Nazneed. "Starting Where the Client Is: An Empirical Investigation." *Social Casework* 60 (February 1979).

Krill, Donald. "Family Interviewing as an Intake Diagnostic Method." *Social Work* 13 (April 1968).

Overall, Betty, and Aronson, H. "Expectations of Psychotherapy in Patients of Lower Socioeconomic Class." *American Journal of Orthopsychiatry* 33 (April 1963).

Perlman, Helen. "Intake and Some Role Considerations." *Social Casework* 41 (April 1960). Also in Helen Perlman, *Persona: Social Role and Personality*. Chicago: University of Chicago Press, 1968.
————. "Some Notes on the Waiting List." *Social Casework* 44 (April 1963).
Petropoulas, Alice. "Intake and Referral in an Alcoholism Agency." *Social Casework* 59 (January 1978).
Roberts, Robert, and Nee, Robert, eds. *Theories of Social Casework*. Chicago: University of Chicago Press, 1970.
Rolfe, Silverman. "A Re-examination of the Intake Procedure." *Social Casework* (December 1970).
Rosenblatt, Aaron. "The Application of Role Concepts to the Intake Process." *Social Casework* 43 (January 1962).
Scherz, Frances. "Intake: Concept and Process." *Social Casework* 33 (June 1952).
Schinke, Steven et al. "Developing Intake-Interviewing Skills." *Social Work Research and Abstracts* 16 (Winter 1980).
Silverman, Phyllis. "A Re-examination of the Intake Procedure." *Social Casework* 51 (December 1970).
Stark, Frances. "Barriers to Client-Worker Communication at Intake." *Social Casework* 40 (April 1959).
Worby, Marsha, and Steinitz, Elaine. "The Telephone Intake: Engaging the Family in Treatment." *Social Casework* 57 (May 1976).

E. CONTRACT (INCLUDING FEES)

Beall, Lyneth. "The Corrupt Contract: Problems in Conjoint Therapy with Parents and Children." *American Journal of Orthopsychiatry* 42 (January 1972).
Claburn, W. Eugene, and Magura, Stephen. "Letter on "Contracting." *Social Work* 22 (May 1977).
Dillon, Carolyn. "A Study of Goal Formulation and Implementation." *Smith College Studies in Social Work* 37 (June 1968).
Estes, Richard, and Henry, Sue. "The Therapeutic Contract in Work with Groups: A Formal Analysis." *Social Service Review* 50 (December 1976).

Frey, Louise, and Meyer, Marguerite. "Exploration and Working Agreement in Two Social Work Methods." In *Exploration in Group Work*. Edited by Saul Bernstein. Boston: Boston University School of Social Work Publications, 1965.

Gabriel, Estelle, and Davids, Morris. "Fees: What Role Do They Play in Treatment?" *Clinical Social Work Journal* 2 (Spring 1974).

Goldberg, Gale. "Structural Approach to Practice: A New Model." *Social Work* 19 (March 1974).

Gottlieb, Werner, and Stanley, Joe. "Mutual Goals and Goal Setting in Casework." *Social Casework* 48 (October 1967).

Lessor, Richard, and Lutkus, Anita. "Two Techniques for the Social Work Practitioner." *Social Work* 16 (January 1971).

Maluccio, Anthony, and Marlow, Wilma. "The Case for the Contract." *Social Work* 19 (January 1974).

Perlman, Helen. *Social Casework: A Problem Solving Process*. Chicago: University of Chicago Press, 1957. See especially Chap. 8, "Person, Problem, Place and Process in the Beginning Phase." See also Chap. 9, "Content in the Beginning Phase."

Pincus, Allen, and Minahan, Anne. *Social Work Practice: Model and Method*. Itasca, Ill.: F.E. Peacock Publishing, 1973. See Chap. 9, "Negotiating Contracts."

Promislo, Estelle. "Confidentiality and Privileged Communication." *Social Work* 24 (January 1979).

Rhodes, Sonya. "Contract Negotiation in the Initial Stage of Casework Service." *Social Service Review* 51 (March 1977).

Rothery, Michael. "Contracts and Contracting." *Clinical Social Work Journal* 8 (Fall 1980).

Sax, Patricia. "An Inquiry into Fee Setting and Its Determinants." *Clinical Social Work Journal* 6 (Winter 1978).

Schubert, Margaret. *Interviewing in Social Work Practice: An Introduction*. New York: Council on Social Work Education, 1971. See Chap. 2, "Getting Started: The Concept of a Contract."

Seabury, Brett. "The Contract: Uses, Abuses, and Limitations." *Social Work* 21 (January 1976).

Shireman, Joan. "Client and Worker Opinions About Fee-Charging in a Child Welfare Agency." *Child Welfare* 54 (May 1975).

Siporin, Max. *Introduction to Social Work Practice*. New York: Macmillan, 1975.

Stein, Theodore; Gambrill, Eileen; and Kermit, Wiltse. "Contracts and Outcomes in Foster Care." *Social Work* 22 (March 1977).

_____. "Foster Care: The Use of Contracts." *Public Welfare* 32 (Fall 1974).

Tropp, Emanuel. "Expectation, Performance and Accountability." *Social Work* 19 (March 1974).

Wilson, Suanna. *Confidentiality in Social Work: Issues and Principles*. New York: The Free Press, 1978.

F. EXPLORATION AND ASSESSMENT—PSYCHOSOCIAL DIAGNOSIS

1. ASSESSMENT PROCESS

Alperin, Richard. "Social Work Has a Problem: A Psychosocial Study." *Clinical Social Work Journal* 5 (Summer 1977).

Argyle, Michael. *Bodily Communication*. New York: International Universities Press, 1975.

Blake, Wilma. "The Influence of Race on Diagnosis." *Smith College Studies in Social Work* 43 (June 1973).

Bloom, Martin. "Challenge to the Helping Professions and the Response of Scientific Practice." *Social Service Review* 52 (December 1978).

Bloom, Mary. "Usefulness of the Home Visit for Diagnosis and Treatment." *Social Casework* 54 (February 1973).

Chapman, Margery. "Salient Need—A Casework Compass." *Social Casework* 58 (June 1977).

Davies, Martin. "The Assessment of Environment in Social Work Research." *Social Casework* 55 (January 1974).

Deykin, Eva. "Life Functioning in Families of Delinquent Boys: An Assessment Model." *Social Service Review* 46 (March 1972).

Diagnostic and Statistical Manual of Mental Disorders (DSM III), 3d ed. Washington, D.C.: American Psychiatric Association, 1980.

Dohrenwend, Bruce. "Notes on Psychosocial Diagnosis." *American Journal of Orthopsychiatry* 41 (October 1971).

Doremus, Bertha. "The Four R's: Social Diagnosis in Health Care." *Health and Social Work* 1 (November 1976).

Germain, Carel. "Social Study: Past and Future." *Social Casework* 49 (July 1968).

Hallowitz, David, and Cutter, Albert. "A Collaborative Diagnostic and Treatment Process with Parents." *Social Work* 3 (July 1958).

Hellenbrand, Shirley. "Client Value Orientation: Implications for Diagnosis and Treatment." *Social Casework* 42 (April 1961). And in *Differential Diagnosis and Treatment in Social Work*. Edited by Francis J. Turner. New York: The Free Press, 1968, and 2d ed., 1976.

Hess, Peg, and Howard, Tina. "An Ecological Model for Assessing Psychosocial Difficulties in Children." *Child Welfare* 60 (September-October 1981).

Hollis, Florence. "Personality Diagnosis in Casework." In *Ego Psychology and Dynamic Casework: Papers from the Smith College for Social Work*. Edited by Howard Parad. New York: Family Service Association of America, 1958.

Kadushin, Alfred. "Diagnosis and Evaluation for (Almost) All Occasions." *Social Work* 8 (January 1963).

Lehrman, Louis. "The Logic of Diagnosis." *Social Casework* 35 (May 1954).

Levinson, Daniel. *The Seasons of a Man's Life*. Chicago: Alfred A. Knopf, 1978.

Levy, Charles. "Labelling: The Social Worker's Responsibility." *Social Casework* 62 (June 1981).

Mullen, Edward. "The Relation Between Diagnosis and Treatment in Casework." *Social Casework* 50 (April 1969).

Ostrower, Ronald. "Study Diagnosis and Treatment: A Conceptual Structure." *Social Casework* 7 (October 1962).

Perlman, Helen. "Diagnosis Anyone?" *Psychiatry and Social Science Review* 43 (December 1969).

———. "In Quest of Coping." *Social Casework* 56 (April 1975).

Peterson, K. Jean. "Assessment in the Life Model: A Historical Perspective." *Social Casework* 60 (December 1979).

Roth, Frederick. "A Practice Regimen for Diagnosis and Treatment of Child Abuse." *Child Welfare* 54 (April 1975).

Scherz, Frances. "Exploring the Use of Family Interviews in Diagnosis. *Social Casework* 45 (April 1964).

Scheunemann, Yolanda, and French, Betty. "Diagnosis as the Foundation of Professional Service." *Social Casework* 55 (March 1974).

Siporin, Max. "Situational Assessment and Intervention." *Social Casework* 53 (February 1972).

Social Work Research and Abstracts. Special Issue on Assessment. 17 (Spring 1981). Especially Austin, Carol. "Client Assessment in Context"; and Levitt, John, and Reid, William. "Rapid-assessment Instruments for Practice."

Spitzer, Robert; Williams, Janet; and Skodol, Andrew. "DSM III: The Major Achievements and an Overview." *American Journal of Psychiatry* 137 (February 1980).

Star, Barbara et al. "Psychosocial Aspects of Wife Battering." *Social Casework* 60 (October 1979).

Weick, Ann. "Reframing the Person-in-Environment Perspective." *Social Work* 26 (March 1981).

Williams, Janet. "DSM III: A Comprehensive Approach to Diagnsosis." *Social Work* 26 (March 1981).

2. SOCIAL AND ECONOMIC FACTORS

Aronson, H., and Overall, Betty. "Treatment Expectations of Patients in Two Social Classes." *Social Work* 11 (January 1966).

Bradbury, Katharine et al. "Public Assistance, Female Headship, and Economic Well-Being." *Journal of Marriage and the Family* 41 (August 1979).

Bryant, Carl. "Introducing Students to the Treatment of Inner-City Families." *Social Casework* 61 (December 1980).

Cade, Brian. "Therapy with Low Socio-Economic Families." *Social Work Today* 6 (May 1975).

Fantl, Bertha. "Casework in Lower Class Districts." In *Differential Diagnosis and Treatment in Social Work*. Edited by Francis J. Turner. New York: The Free Press, 1968, and 2d ed., 1976.

Fischer, Joel, and Miller, Henry. "The Effect of Client Race and Social Class on Clinical Judgments." *Clinical Social Work Journal* 1:2 (Summer 1973).

Garrison, John, and Werfel, Sandra. "A Network Approach to Clinical Social Work." *Clinical Social Work Journal* 5 (Summer 1977).

Giovannoni, Jeanne, and Billingsley, Andrew. "Child Neglect Among the Poor: A Study of Parental Adequacy in Families of Three Ethnic Groups." *Child Welfare* 49 (April 1970).

Graff, Harold; Kenig, Lana; and Radaff, Geoffrey. "Prejudice of Upper Class Therapists Against Lower Class Patients." *Psychiatric Quarterly* 45 (1971). Also in James Goodman, ed. *Dynamics of Racism in Social Work Practice*. Washington, D.C.: National Association of Social Workers, 1973.

Hallowitz, David. "Counselling and Treatment of the Poor Black Family." *Social Casework* 56 (October 1975).

Jones, Enrico. "Social Class and Psychotherapy: "A Critical Review of Research." *Psychiatry* 37 (November 1974).

Kaslow, Florence. "How Relevant is Family Counseling in Public Welfare Settings?" *Public Welfare* 30 (Fall 1972).

Lewis, Ronald, and Ho, Man Keung. "Social Work with Native Americans." *Social Work* 20 (September 1975).

Lurie, Olga. "Parents' Attitudes Toward Use of Mental Health Services: Socio-Economic Differences." *American Journal of Orthopsychiatry* 44 (January 1974).

McKay, Elizabeth. "Social Work With the Wealthy." *Social Casework* 57 (April 1976).

Mayer, John, and Rosenblatt, Aaron. "The Client's Social Context: Its Effect on Continuance in Treatment." *Social Casework* 45 (November 1964).

Mayer, John, and Timms, Noel, eds. "Clash in Perspective Between Worker and Client." *Social Casework*. London: Routledge and Kegan Paul, 1970.

————. *The Client Speaks: Working Class Impressions of Casework*. Chicago: Aldine Publishing, 1970.

Miller, Donna. "Influence of Sex on Clinical Judgement." *Smith College Studies in Social Work* 44 (February 1974).

Minuchin, Salvador. "Techniques for Working with Disorganized Low Socio-economic Families." *American Journal of Orthopsychiatry* 37 (October 1967).

Orcutt, Ben. "Casework Intervention and the Problems of the Poor." *Social Casework* 54 (February 1973).

————, ed. *Poverty and Social Casework Services*. Metuchen, N.J.: Scarecrow Press, 1974.

Peterson, Roger. "Social Class, Social Learning and Wife Abuse." *Social Service Review* 54 (September 1980).

Pierson, Arthur. "Social Work Techniques with the Poor." *Social Casework* 51 (October 1970).

Polansky, Norman, and Williams, David. "Class Orientations to Child Neglect." *Social Work* 23 (September 1978).
Rodman, Lillian. *Worlds of Pain: Life in the Working Class Family.* New York: Basic Books. 1976.
Schneiderman, Leonard. "Social Class Diagnosis and Treatment." *American Journal of Orthopsychiatry* 35 (January 1965).
Stiles, Evelyn. "Hear It Like It Is." *Social Casework* 53 (May 1972).
Willie, Charles. "The Black Family and Social Class." *American Journal of Orthopsychiatry* 44 (January 1974).

3. RACIAL, ETHNIC, AND CULTURAL FACTORS

See related items under Minorities.

Abad, Vicente et al. "A Model for Delivery of Mental Health Services to Spanish-speaking Minorities." *American Journal of Orthopsychiatry* 44 (July 1974).
Allen, Josephine, and Burwell, Yolanda. "Ageism and Racism: Two Issues Social Work Education and Practice." *Journal of Education for Social Work* 16 (Spring 1980).
"Asian and Pacific Islander Americans." *Social Casework* 57 (March 1976). Entire issue on Asian and Pacific Islander Americans.
Banks, George. "The Effects of Race on One-to-One Helping Interviews." *Social Service Review* 45 (June 1971).
Blake, Wilma. "The Influence of Race on Diagnosis." *Smith College Studies in Social Work* 43 (June 1973).
Bloch, Julia. "The White Worker and the Negro Client in Psychotherapy." *Social Work* 13 (April 1968).
Bowles, Dorcas. "Making Casework Relevant to Black People: Approaches, Techniques, Theoretical Implications." *Child Welfare* 48 (October 1969).
Brayboy, Thomas, and Marks, Malcolm. "Transference Variations Evoked by Racial Differences." *American Journal of Psychotherapy* 22:3 (July 1968). Also in *Dynamics of Racism in Social Work Practice.* Edited by James Goodman. Washington, D.C.: National Association of Social Workers, 1973.
Brennan, Jere, comp. *The Forgotten American—American Indians Remembered: A Selected Bibliography for Use in Social Work and Education.* New York: Council on Social Work Education, 1972.

Cade, Toni, ed. *The Black Woman: An Anthology*. New York: Signet, 1970.

Cafferty, Pastora, and Chestang, Leon, eds. *The Diverse Society*. Washington, D.C.: National Association of Social Workers, 1976.

Cameron, J. Talavera. "An Advocacy Program for Spanish-Speaking People." *Social Casework* 57 (July 1976).

Carter, James, and Haizlip, Thomas. "Race and Its Relevance to Transference." *American Journal of Orthopsychiatry* 42 (October 1972). Also in Goodman's *Dynamics of Racism in Social Work Practice*.

Chandler, Susan. "Self-Perceived Competency in Cross-Cultural Counseling." *Social Casework* 61 (June 1980).

Cohen, Jerome. *Race as a Factor in Social Work Practice*. Edited by Roger Miller. New York: National Association of Social Workers, 1969. Also in Goodman's *Dynamics of Racism in Social Work Practice*.

Cole, J. Pulisul. "Differences in the Provision of Mental Health Services by Race." *American Journal of Orthopsychiatry* 46 (July 1976).

"Contra Viento y Marea: Against the Stormy Seas." *Social Casework* 55 (February 1974). Entire issue on Puerto Rican culture.

Cooper, Shirley. "A Look at the Effect of Racism on Clinical Work." *Social Casework* 54 (February 1973). Also in Goodman's *Dynamics of Racism in Social Work Practice*.

Delgado, Melvin. "Herbal Medicine in the Puerto Rican Community." *Health and Social Work* 4 (May 1979).

Dunmore, Charlotte, comp. *Poverty, Participation, Protest, Power and Black Americans: A Selected Bibliography for Use in Social Work Education*. New York: Council on Social Work Education, 1970.

Ghali, Sonia. "Culture Sensitivity and the Puerto Rican Client." *Social Casework* 58 (October 1977).

Gitterman, Alex, and Schaeffer, Alice. "The White Professional and the Black Client." *Social Casework* 53 (May 1972). Also in Goodman's *Dynamics of Racism in Social Work Practice*. (See entry below.)

Goodman, James. "Racial Minorities in the 1980s" *Social Work* 19 (September 1974).

_____, ed. *Dynamics of Racism in Social Work Practice*. Washington, D.C.: National Associatio of Social Workers, 1973.

Hanson, Barbara. "Black Process in Clinically Depressed Women: A Conceptual Framework for Practice." *Clinical Social Work Journal* 2 (Fall 1974).

Ho, Man Keung. "Social Work with Asian Americans." *Social Casework* 57 (March 1976).

Institute of Puerto Rican Studies, Brooklyn College. *The Puerto Rican People: A Selected Bibliography for Use in Social Work Education*. New York: Council on Social Work Education, 1973.

Jacobson, Doris. "The Influence of Cultural Identification on Family Behavior." *Social Service Review* 46 (September 1972).

Kadushin, Alfred. "The Racial Factor in the Interview." *Social Work* 17 (May 1972).

Kitano, Harry, comp. *Asians in America: A Selected Bibliography for Use in Social Work Education*. New York: Council on Social Work Education, 1971.

"La Causa Chicana: The Movement for Justice." *Social Casework* 52 (May 1971). Entire issue on Chicanos.

Lazare, Aron et al. "Disposition Decisions in a Walk-in Clinic: Social Psychiatric Variables." *American Journal of Orthopsychiatry* 46 (July 1976).

Lide, Pauline. "Dialogue on Racism: A Prologue to Action?" *Social Casework* 52 (July 1971).

Logan, Sadye. "Race, Identity, and Black Children: A Developmental Perspective." *Social Casework* 62 (January 1981).

Mangold, Margaret, ed. *La Causa Chicana: The Movement for Justice*. New York: Family Service Association of America, 1972.

Mendes, Helen. "Countertransferences and Counterculture Clients." *Social Casework* 58 (March 1977).

Mindel, Charles, and Habenstein, Robert. *Ethnic Families in America: Patterns and Variations*. 2d ed. New York: Elsevier North-Holland, 1981.

Mizio, Emelicia. Puerto Rican Social Workers and Racism." *Social Casework* 53 (May 1972).

Navarro, Eliseo, comp. *The Chicano Community: A Selected Bibliography for Use in Social Work Education*. New York: Council on Social Work Education, 1971.

Petro, Olive, and French, Betty. "The Black Client's View of Himself." *Social Casework* 53 (October 1972).

"The Phoenix from the Flame: The American Indian Today." *Social Casework* 61 (October 1980). Entire issue on the American Indian.

Pinderhughes, Elaine. "Teaching Empathy in Cross-Cultural Social Work." *Social Work* 24 (July 1979).

Sager, Clifford; Brayboy, Thomas; and Waxenberg, Barbara. "Black Patient—White Therapist." *American Journal of Orthopsychiatry* 42 (April 1972).

Shannon, Barbara. "The Impact of Racism on Personality Development." *Social Casework* 54 (November 1973).

Siegel, Jerome. "A Brief Review of the Effects of Race in Clinical Service Interactions." *American Journal of Orthopsychiatry* 44 (July 1974).

Social Casework. Entire issue on blacks and racism. 51 (May 1970).

———. Entire issue on ethnic and racial issues in the delivery of social services. 53 (May 1972).

Tuck, Sam, Jr. "Working with Black Fathers." *American Journal of Orthopsychiatry* 41 (April 1971).

Willie, Charles. "The Black Family and Social Class." *American Journal of Orthopsychiatry* 44 (January 1974).

4. SOCIAL FUNCTIONING (INCLUDING SEXUAL FUNCTIONING)

a. Role Considerations

Alexander, Jannette. "Alternative Life Styles: Relationship Between New Realities and Practice." *Clinical Social Work Journal* 4 (Winter 1976).

Biddle, Bruce, and Thomas, Edwin. *Role Theory*. New York: John Wiley and Sons, 1966.

Blanck, Gertrude, and Blanck, Rubin. *Marriage and Personality Development*. New York: Columbia University Press, 1968.

Chescheir, Martha. "Social Role Discrepancies as Clues to Practice." *Social Work* 24 (March 1979).

Einzig, Judith. "The Child Within: A Study of Expectant Fatherhood." *Smith College Studies in Social Work* 50 (March 1980).

Fisher, Lawrence, and Warren, Robert. "The Concept of Role Assignment in Family Therapy." *International Journal of Group Psychotherapy* 22 (January 1972).

Gochros, Harvey, and Schultz, Leroy. *Human Sexuality and Social Work*. New York: Association Press, 1972.

Group for the Advancement of Psychiatry. Report no. 88. *Assessment of Sexual Function: A Guide to Interviewing*. New York: Group for the Advancement of Psychiatry, 1973.

Harris, Linda, and Lucas, Margaret. "Sex Role Stereotyping." *Social Work* 20 (September 1976).

Hersle, Alexander. "Changes in Family Functioning Following Placement of a Retarded Child." *Social Work* 15 (October 1970).

Lipman-Blumen, Jean. "The Implications for Family Structure of Changing Sex Roles." *Social Casework* 57 (February 1976).

Longres, John, and Bailey, Robert. "Men's Issues and Sexism: A Journal Review." *Social Work* 24 (January 1979).

McBroom, Elizabeth. "Socialization and Social Casework." In *Theories of Social Casework*. Edited by Robert Roberts and Robert Nee. Chicago: University of Chicago Press, 1970.

Maglin, Arthur. "Sex Role Differences in Heroin Addiction." *Social Casework* 55 (March 1974).

Mendes, Helen. "Single Fatherhood." *Social Work* 21 (July 1976).

"Modern Sexuality." Special issue of *Clinical Social Work Journal* (Winter 1973).

Perlman, Helen. "Intake and Some Role Considerations." In *Social Casework in the Fifties*. Edited by Cora Kasius. New York: Family Service Association of America, 1962.

————. *Persona: Social Role and Personality*. Chicago: University of Chicago Press, 1968.

Pleck, Joseph. "Prisoners of Manliness. *Psychology Today* 15 (September 1981).

Sherman, Sanford. "The Therapist and Changing Sex Roles." *Social Casework* 57 (February 1976).

Strean, Herbert. "Role Theory." In *Social Work Treatment: Interlocking Theoretical Approaches*. Edited by Francis J. Turner. New York: The Free Press, 1974.

————. "Role Theory, Role Models and Casework: Review of the Literature and Practice Applications." *Social Work* 12 (April 1967).

Varley, Barbara. "The Use of Role Theory in the Treatment of Disturbed Adolescents." *Social Casework* 49 (June 1968).

Wolman, Benjamin, and Money, John, eds. *Handbook of Human Sexuality*. Englewood Cliffs, N.J.: Prenctice-Hall, 1980.

b. Use of Ego Psychology

Bandler, Bernard. "The Concept of Ego-Supportive Psychotherapy." In *Ego-Oriented Casework: Problems and Pespectives.* Edited by Howard Parad and Roger Miller. New York: Family Service Association of America, 1963.

Bandler, Louise. "Casework—A Process of Socialization: Gains, Limitations, Conclusions. " In *The Drifters: Children of Disorganized Lower-Class Families.* Edited by Eleanor Pavenstedt. Boston: Little, Brown and Co., 1967.

————. "Some Casework Aspects of Ego Growth Through Sublimation." In Parad's and Miller's *Ego-Oriented Casework: Problems and Perspectives.* (See entry under Bandler above.)

Bennett, Joy. "Use of Ego Psychology Concepts in Family Service Intake." *Social Casework* 54 (May 1973).

Blanck, Gertrude, and Blanck, Rubin. *Ego Psychology: Theory and Practice.* New York: Columbia University Press, 1974.

————. *Ego Psychology II: Psychoanalytic Developmental Psychology.* New York: Columbia University Press, 1979.

Cath, Stanley. "Some Dynamics of the Middle and Later Years." In *Crisis Intervention: Selected Readings.* Edited by Howard J. Parad. New York: Family Service Association of America, 1965.

Cummings, John, and Cummings, Elaine. *Ego and Milieu.* New York: Atherton Press, 1966.

Denadello, Gloria. "Some Applications of Ego Psychology Theory to Practice and Programs in Child Welfare." *Child Welfare* 46 (November 1967).

Edwards, David. "Shame and Pain and 'Shut Up or I'll Really Give You Something to Cry About.' " *Clinical Social Work Journal* 4 (Spring 1976).

Ford, Caroline. "Ego Adaptive Mechanisms of Older People." *Social Casework* 46 (January 1965).

Garrett, Annette. "Modern Casework: The Contribution of Ego Psychology." In *Ego Psychology and Dynamic Casework: Papers from the Smith College for Social Work.* Edited by Howard Parad. New York: Family Service Association of America, 1958.

Germain, Carel. "General Systems Theory and Ego Psychology: An Ecological Perspective." *Social Service Review* 52 (December 1978).

Green, Sidney. "Psychoanalytic Contributions to Casework Treatment of Marital Problems." *Social Casework* 35 (December 1954).

Kaufman, Irving. "Psychodynamics of Protective Casework." In Parad's and Miller's *Ego-Oriented Casework: Problems and Perspectives*. (See entry under Bandler, above.)

Kernberg, Otto. Borderline Personality Organization." *Journal of American Psychoanalytic Association* 15 (July 1967).

————. "The Treatment of Patients with Borderline Personality Organization." *International Journal of Psychoanalysis* 49 (1968).

Lazarus, Richard. *Psychological Stress and the Coping Process*. New York: McGraw Hill, 1966.

Lipschitz, Joseph. "A Brief Review of Psychoanalytic Ego Psychology." *Social Casework* 45 (January 1964).

Lloyd, Katherine. "Helping A Child Adapt to Stress: The Use of Ego Psychology in Casework." *Social Service Review* 31 (March 1957).

Loewenstein, Sophie. "Inner and Outer Space in Social Casework." *Social Casework* 60 (January 1979).

Mahler, Margaret. *On Human Symbiosis and the Vicissitudes of Individuation*. New York: International Universities Press, 1968.

Oxley, Genevieve. "A Life Model Approach to Change." *Social Casework* 52 (December 1971).

Panter, Ethel. "Ego Building Procedures that Foster Social Functioning." *Social Casework* 47 (March 1966).

Parad, Howard, ed. *Ego Psychology and Dynamic Casework*. New York: Family Service Association of America, 1958.

————, and Miller, Roger, eds. *Ego-Oriented Casework: Problems and Perspectives*. New York: Family Service Association of America, 1963.

Polansky, Norman. *Ego Psychology and Communication Theory for the Interview*. New York: Atherton Press, 1971.

Simon, Bernece. *Relationship Between Theory and Practice in Social Casework: Ego Assessment and Ego Supportive Casework Treatment*. Monograph no. 4. New York: National Association of Social Workers, 1960.

Stamm, Isabel. "Ego Psychology in the Emerging Theoretical Base of Casework." In *Issues in American Social Work*. Edited by Alfred Kahn. New York: Columbia University Press, 1959.

Stevenson, Elizabeth. "Casework Treatment of Parent Child Conflicts." *Social Casework* 49 (December 1968).

Taylor, Ronald. "Psychosexual Development Among Black Children and Youth: A Reexamination." *American Journal of Orthopsychiatry* 46 (January 1976).

Upham, Frances. *Ego Analysis in the Helping Professions*. New York: Family Service Association of America, 1973.

Wasserman, Sidney. "Ego Psychology." In *Social Work Treatment: Interlocking Theoretical Approaches*. Edited by Francis Turner. New York: The Free Press, 1974.

White, Robert. "Ego Reality in Psychoanalytic Theory." *Psychological Issues* 3 (1963).

Widem, Paul. "Some Dimensions of Ego Continuity in Social Casework." *Social Work* 11 (October 66).

Wood, Katherine. "The Contribution of Psychoanalysis and Ego Psychology to Social Casework." In *Social Casework: Theories in Action*. Edited by Herbert Strean. Metuchen, N.J.: Scarecrow Press, 1971.

5. FAMILY ASSESSMENT

See related items under Family Treatment.

Ackerman, Nathan, ed. *Expanding Theory and Practice in Family Therapy*. New York: Family Service Association of America, 1967.

————. *Exploring the Base for Family Therapy*. New York: Family Service Association of America, 1961.

————. *Family Process*. New York: Basic Books, 1970.

Ahrons, Constance. "Redefining the Divorced Family: A Conceptual Framework." *Social Work* 25 (November 1980).

Anderson, Carol. "Family Communication: Words, Messages and Meanings." *Smith College Studies in Social Work* 49 (March 1979).

Anthony, James, and Benedeck, Therese. *Parenthood: Its Psychology and Pschopathology*. Boston: Little, Brown and Co., 1970.

Ball, Margaret. "Issues of Violence in Family Casework." *Social Casework* 58 (January 1977).

Bardill, Donald, and Ryan, Francis. *Family Group Casework: A Casework Approach to Family Therapy*. Washington, D.C.: Metropolitan Chapter of the National Association of Social Workers, 1969.

Beatman, Frances. "Family Interaction: Its Significance for Diagnosis and Treatment." *Social Casework* 38 (March 1957). Also in *Social Casework–The Fifties: Selected Articles 1950–1960*. Edited by Cora Kasius. New York: Family Service Association of America, 1962.

34

_____. "The Training and Preparation of Workers for Family-Group Treatment." *Social Casework* 45 (April 1964).

Blanck, Rubin. "Marriage as a Phase of Personality Development." *Social Casework* 48 (March 1967).

Bowen, Murray, "The Family as the Unit of Study and Treatment." *American Journal of Orthopsychiatry* 31 (January 1961).

Canton, Lucile. "Clinical Issues in Domestic Violence." *Social Casework* 62 (January 1981).

Chiancola, Samuel. "The Process of Separation and Divorce: A New Approach." *Social Casework* 59 (October 1978).

Cromwell, Ronald et al. "Tools and Techniques for Diagnosis and Evaluation in Marital and Family Therapy." *Family Process* 15 (March 1976).

Framo, James. "Personal Reflections of a Family Therapist." *Journal of Marriage and Family Counseling* 1 (January 1975).

Freeman, Henry. "Applying Family Diagnosis in Practice." In *Casework with Families and Children*. Edited by Eileen Younghusband. Chicago: University of Chicago Press, 1965.

Gomberg, Robert. "Family Diagnosis: Trends in Theory and Practice." In Younghusband's *Casework with Families and Children*. (See entry under Freeman above.)

Group for the Advancement of Psychiatry. Report no. 78. *Treatment of Families in Conflict*. New York: Science House, 1970.

Hartman, Ann. "Diagrammatic Assessment of Family Relationships." *Social Casework* 59 (October 1978).

_____. "The Family: A Central Focus for Practice." *Social Work* 26 (January 1981).

Hill, Reuben. "Generic Features of Families Under Stress." In *Crisis Intervention: Selected Readings*. Edited by Howard Parad. New York: Family Service Association of America, 1965.

Hudson, Walter, and Glisson, Dianne. "Assessment of Marital Discord in Social Work Practice." *Social Service Review* 50 (June 1976).

Hudson, Walter et al. "Assessing Discord in Family Relationships." *Social Work Research and Abstracts* 16 (Fall 1980).

Jackson, Doris. "Stepfamilies: Myths and Realities." *Social Work* 24 (May 1979).

Johnson, Harriette. "Working with Stepfamilies: Principles of Practice." *Social Work* 25 (July 1980).

Justice, Blair, and Justice, Rita. *The Abusing Family*. New York: Human Sciences Press, 1976.

Kaplan, Barbara. "Understanding Family Disruption: The Cognitive Development of Children." *Social Service Review* 54 (September 1980).

Krill, Donald. "Family Interviewing as an Intake Diagnostic Method." *Social Work* 13 (April 1968).

Laing, R.D. *The Politics of the Family*. New York: Pantheon, 1971.

Levande, Diane. "Family Therory as a Necessary Component of Family Therapy." *Social Casework* 57 (May 1976).

Lewis, Jerry et al. *No Single Thread*. New York: Brunner/Mazel, 1976.

Lipman-Blumen, Jean. "The Implications for Family Structure of Changing Sex Roles." *Social Casework* 57 (February 1976).

Mendes, Helen. "Single-Parent Families: A Typology of Life Styles." *Social Work* 24 (May 1979).

Minuchin, Salvador. "The Plight of the Poverty Stricken Family in the United States." *Child Welfare* 49 (March 1970).

_____ et al. *Families of the Slums/Exploration of Their Structure and Treatment*. New York: Basic Books. 1967.

Nagy-Boszormenyi, Ivan, and Framo, J.L., eds. *Intensive Family Therapy*. New York: Harper and Row, 1965.

O'Connell, Patricia. "Developmental Tasks of the Family." *Smith College Studies in Social Work* 2 (June 1972).

Papajohn, John, and Spiegel, John. *Transactions in Families*. San Francisco: Jossey-Bass, 1975.

Pfouts, Jane. "The Sibling Relationship: A Forgotten Dimension." *Social Work* 21 (May 1976).

Rapoport, Rhona. "Normal Crises, Family Structure and Mental Health." *Family Process* 2 (March 1963). Also in Parad's *Crisis Intervention*. (See entry under Hill above.)

Rhodes, Sonya. "A Developmental Approach to the Life Cycle of the Family." *Social Casework* 58 (May 1977).

Sacklin, H. David, and Raffe, Irving. "Multi-Problem Families: A Social Psychological Perspective." *Clinical Social Work Journal* 4:1 (Spring 1976).

Scherz, Frances. "The Crisis of Adolescence in Family Life." *Social Casework* 48 (April 1967).

_____. "Family Therapy." In *Theories of Social Casework*. Edited by Robert Roberts and Robert Nee. Chicago: University of Chicago Press, 1970.

Schulman, Gerda. "Myths That Intrude on the Adaptation of the Step-Family." *Social Casework* 53 (March 1972).
Skynner, A. C. Robin. *Systems of Family and Marital Psychotherapy.* New York: Brunner/Mazel, 1976.
Startz, Morton, and Evans, Claire. "Developmental Phases of Marriage and Marital Therapy." *Social Casework* 62 (June 1981).
Visher, Emily, and Visher, John. "Common Problems of Stepparents and Their Spouses." *American Journal of Orthopsychiatry* 48 (April 1978).
Wald, Esther. *The Remarried Family: Challenge and Promise.* New York: Family Service Association of America, 1981.
Walker, Kenneth; Rogers, Joy; and Messinger, Lillian. "Remarriage After Divorce: A Review." *Social Casework* 58 (May 1977).
Walker, Libby et al. "An Annotated Bibliography of the Remarried, the Living Together, and Their Children." *Family Process* 18 (June 1979).

6. CLINICAL DIAGNOSIS

Stone, Alan, and Stone, Sue, eds. *The Abnormal Personality Through Literature.* Englewood Cliffs, N.J.: Prentice-Hall, 1966.

a. Psychosis
Arieti, Silvano. "The Psychodynamics of Schizophrenia." *American Journal of Psychotherapy* 22 (July 1968).
Cain, Lillian. "Preparing a Psychotic Patient for Major Surgery." *Social Casework* 55 (July 1974).
Cameron, Norman. *Personality Development and Psychopathology.* New York: Houghton Mifflin, 1968.
Christmas, June. "Socio-Psychiatric Treatment of Disadvantaged Psychotic Adults." *American Journal of Orthopsychiatry* 37 (January 1967).
Cunningham, Murry et al. "Community Placement of Released Mental Patients: A Five-Year Study." *Social Work* 14 (January 1969).
Edward, Joyce. "The Therapist as a Catalyst in Promoting Separation-Individuation." *Clinical Social Work Journal* 4 (Fall 1976).

Farber, Laura. "Casework Treatment of Ambulatory Schizophrenics." *Social Casework* 39 (January 1958). Also in *Differential Diagnosis and Treatment in Social Work*. Edited by Francis Turner. New York: The Free Press, 1968, 2d ed. 1976.

Freuert, Patricia, and Ellis, David. "Treating the Young Adult Schizophrenic Patient." *Social Casework* 46 (December 1965).

Green, Hannah. *I Never Promised You a Rose Garden*. New York: Signet Books, 1964.

Hall, Julian, and Bradley, Anna. "Treating Long-term Mental Patients." *Social Work* 20 (September 1975).

Hankoff, L., and Galvin, John. "Psychopharmacological Treatment and Its Implications for Social Work." *Social Work* 13 (July 1968).

Hatfield, Agnes. "Psychological Costs of Schizophrenia in the Family." *Social Work* 23 (September 1978).

Holzman, Philip. "The Modesty of Nature: A Social Perspective on Schizophrenia." *Social Service Review* 51 (December 1977).

Hyde, Alexander. *Living with Schizophrenia: A Guide for Patients and Their Families*. Chicago: Contemporary Books, 1980.

Laing, R. D. *The Divided Self*. New York: Pantheon Press, 1969.

Livingston, Peter, and Shader, Richard. "Thought Disorder in Schizophrenia." *Social Casework* 49 (October 1968).

Lukton, Rosemary. "Current Views on the Etiology of Schizophrenia." *Health and Social Work* 1 (May 1976).

MacKinnon, Roger, and Michels, Robert. *The Psychiatric Interview in Clinical Practice*. Philadelphia: W. B. Saunders, 1971.

Marcus, Esther. "Ego Breakdown in Schizophrenia, Some Implications for Casework Treatment." *Amercian Journal of Orthopsychiatry* 31 (April 1961). Also in Turner's *Differential Diagnosis and Treatment*. (See entry under Farber above.)

Nelsen, Judith. "Treatment Issues in Schizophrenia." *Social Casework* 56 (March 1975).

_____. "Treatment-planning for Schizophrenia." *Social Casework* 56 (February 1975).

Plath, Sylvia. *The Bell Jar*. New York: Harper and Row, 1971.

Raymond, Margaret; Slaby, Andrew; and Lieb, Julian. "Familial Responses to Mental Illness." *Social Casework* 56 (October 1975).

Roueché, Berton. "Electric Shock Therapy: Annals of Medicine." *New Yorker*, 9 September 1974.

Shemberg, Kenneth, and Leventhal, Donald. "Outpatient Treatment of Schizophrenic Students in a University Clinic." *Bulletin of the Menninger Clinic* 36 (November 1972).
"Society and Insanity." Entire issue of *Clinical Social Work* 2 (Winter 1974).
"Special Report: Schizophrenia." *Schizophrenic Bulletin* 2 (1976).
Varley, Barbara. "Reaching Out Therapy with Schizophrenic Patients." *American Journal of Orthopsychiatry* 29 (April 1959). Also in Turner's *Differential Diagnosis and Treatment* (See entry under Farber above.)
Vesper, Sue, and Spearman, Frankie. "Treatment of Marital Conflict Resulting from Severe Personality Disturbance." *Social Casework* 47 (November 1966).
Waring, Mary. "Averting Hospitalization for Adult Schizophrenia—A Search for Ameliorative Factors." *Social Work* 11 (October 1966).

b. Character Disorder and Neurotic Character
Adler, Gerald, and Shapiro, Leon. "Some Difficulties in the Treatment of the Aggressive, Acting-Out Patient." *American Journal of Psychotherapy* 27 (October 1973).
Anderson, Lorna, and Shafer, Gretchen. "The Character-Disordered Family: A Community Treatment Model for Family Sexual Abuse." *American Journal of Orthopsychiatry* 49 (July 1979).
Bittermann, Catherine. "Marital Adjustment Patterns of Clients with Compulsive Character Disorders: Implications for Treatment." *Social Casework* 47 (November 1966).
Donnelly, John. "Aspects of the Treatment of Character Disorders." *Archives of General Psychiatry* 15 (July 1966).
Easser, Barbara, and Easser, Stanley. "Hysterical Personality: A Reevaluation." *The Psychoanalytic Quarterly* 34 (July 1965).
Jackel, Merl. "Clients with Character Disorders." *Social Casework* 44:6 (June 1963). Also in *Differential Diagnosis and Treatment in Social Work*. Edited by Francis Turner. New York: The Free Press, 1968, 2d ed. 1976.
Jones, Maxwell. "The Treatment of Character Disorders." In Turner's *Differential Diagnosis and Treatment*.
Leach, Jean. "Casework Techniques in the Treatment of Character Disorder." In *Casework Papers 1956: From the National Conference of Social Welfare*. New York: Family Service Association of America, 1956.

Miller, Robert. "An Oblique Approach to Clients with Behavior Disorders." *Social Work* 10 (April 1965).

Pollak, Otto. "Treatment of Character Disorders: A Dilemma in Casework Culture." *Social Service Review* 35 (June 1961). Also in Turner's *Differential Diagnosis and Treatment*. (See entry under Jackel above.)

————; Young, Hazel; and Leach, Helen. "Differential Diagnosis and Treatment of Character Disturbances." *Social Casework* 41 (December 1960).

Reiner, Beatrice. "Casework Treatment of Sexual Confusion in Character Disorders." *Social Casework* 43 (December 1962). Also in Turner's *Differential Diagnosis and Treatment*. (See entry under Jackel above.)

————, and Kaufman, Irving, *Character Disorders in Parents of Delinquents*. New York: Family Service Association of America, 1959.

Reynolds, Rosemary, and Siegle, Elsa. "A Study of Casework with Sado-Masochistic Marriage Partners." *Social Casework* 40 (December 1959). Also in Turner's *Differential Diagnosis and Treatment*. (See entry under Jackel above.)

Scherz, Frances. "Treatment of Acting-Out Character Disorders in a Marital Problem." In *Casework Papers 1956: From the National Conference of Social Welfare*. New York: Family Service Association of America, 1956.

Sterba, Richard. "On Character Neurosis." In Turner's *Differential Diagnosis and Treatment*. (See Turner entry below.)

Strean, Herbert. "Psychotherapy with the Narcissistic Character Disorder." *Psychotherapy* 9 (Fall 1972).

Turner, Francis. ed. *Differential Diagnosis and Treatment in Social Work*. New York: The Free Press, 1968. 2d ed., 1976.

c. Neurosis

Ackerman, Nathan. "The Diagnosis of Neurotic Martial Interaction." *Social Casework* 35 (April 1954). Also in *Social Casework in the Fifties*. Edited by Cora Kasius. New York: Family Service Association of America, 1963.

Austin, Lucille. "Dynamics and Treatment of the Client with Anxiety Hysteria." In *Ego Psychology and Dynamic Casework: Papers from the Smith College for Social Work*. Edited by Howard Parad. New York: Family Service Association of America, 1958. And in *Differential Diagnosis and Treatment in Social Work*. Edited by Francis Turner. New York: The Free Press, 1968, and 2d ed., 1976.

Boyer, Bryce. "Christmas Neurosis." *Journal of American Psychoanalytic Association* 13 (July 1955).

Brandzel, Esther. "Working Through the Oedipal Struggle in Family Unit Sessions." *Social Casework* 46 (July 1965).

Chodoff, P. "The Diagnosis of Hysteria: An Overview." *American Journal of Psychiatry* 131 (October 1974).

Herowitz, Mardi. *The Hysterical Personality*. New York: Jason Aronson, 1977.

Hunt, Flora. "Initial Treatment of the Client with Anxiety Hysteria: A Case Presentation." In Parad's *Ego Psychology and Dynamic Casework*. (See entry under Austin above.)

Krill, Donald. "Loosening the Oedipal Bind Through Family Therapy." *Social Casework* 48 (November 1967).

Laughlin, Henry. *The Neurosis*. Washington, D.C.: Butterworths, 1967.

Leventhal, Theodore et al. "Therapeutic Strategies with School Phobics." *American Journal of Orthopsychiatry* 37 (January 1967).

Liebman, Ronald et al. "The Role of the Family in the Treatment of Anorexia Nervosa." *Journal of American Academic Child Psychiatry* 13 (February 1974).

Nelsen, Judith. "Treatment of Patients with Minor Psychosomatic Disorders." *Social Casework* 50 (December 1969).

Noonan, J. Robert. "An Obsessive Compulsive Reaction Treated by Induced Anxiety." *American Journal of Psychotherapy* 25 (April 1971).

Perry, Sylvia. "The Conscious Use of Relationship with the Neurotic Client." In Parad's *Ego Psychology and Dynamic Casework*. (See entry under Austin above.)

Powers, Henry. "Psychotherapy for Hysterical Individuals." *Social Casework* 53 (July 1972).

Rosman, Bernice et al. "Family Lunch Session: An Introduction to Family Therapy in Anorexia Nervosa." *American Journal of Orthopsychiatry* 45 (October 1975).

Scarborough, H. E. "The Hypothesis of Hidden Health in the Treatment of Severe Neurosis." *Social Casework* 49 (May 1968).

Shapiro, David. *Neurotic Styles*. New York: Basic Books. 1965.

Suess, James. "Short-Term Psychotherapy with the Compulsive Personality and the Obsessive-Compulsive Neurotic." *American Journal of Psychiatry* 129 (September 1972). Also in Turner's *Differential Diagnosis and Treatment* (See entry under Austin above.)

Walden, Ray. "Neurosis and the Social Structure." *American Journal of Orthopsychiatry* 38 (January 1968).

Wasserman, Sidney. "Casework Treatment of the Neurotic Delinquent Adolescent and the Compulsive Mother. *Social Casework* 43 (November 1962).

d. Depression, Suicide, and Reaction to Death and Dying

Abrams, Ruth. *Not Alone with Cancer: A Guide for Those Who Care; What to Expect; What to Do.* Springfield, Ill.: Charles C Thomas, 1974.

Bennett, A. E. "Recognizing The Potential Suicide." *Geriatrics* 22 (May 1967).

Bowlby, John. *Loss-Sadness and Depression, vol. 3, Attachment and Loss series.* New York: Basic Books, 1980.

Cameron, Norman. *Personality Development and Psychopathology.* New York: Houghton Mifflin Co., 1963. See especially Chap. 18, "Involutional Psychotic Reactions"; and Chap. 12, "Neurotic Depressive Reactions."

Cammer, Leonard. *Up From Depresion.* New York: Simon and Schuster, 1969.

Chrzanowski, G. et al. "Panel Discussion: The Management of Depression in Children and Adults." *Contemporary Psychoanalysis* 2 (January 1965).

Combs, Terri. "A Cognitive Therapy for Depression: Theory, Techniques and Issues," *Social Casework* 61 (June 1980).

Deykin, Eva; Weissman, Myrna; and Klerman, Gerald. "Treatment of Depressed Women." *British Journal of Social Work* (Fall 1971). Also in *Differential Diagnosis and Treatment in Social Work.* Edited by Francis Turner. New York: The Free Press, 1968, 2d ed., 1976.

DuBois, Paul. *The Hospice Way of Death.* New York: Human Sciences Press, 1980.

Engel, G. L. "Is Grief a Disease?" *Psychoanalytic Medicine* 23 (1961).

Figley, Charles. *Stress Disorders Among Vietnam Veterans.* New York: Brunner/Mazel, 1978.

French, Alfred, and Irving, Berlin. *Depression in Children and Adolescents.* New York: Human Sciences Press, 1979.

Glaser, Kurt. "Suicidal Children—Management." *American Journal of Psychotherapy* 25 (January 1971).

Golden, Janet. "Depression in Middle and Late Childhood: Implications for Intervention." *Child Welfare* 60 (July-August 1981).

Goldstein, Eda. "Social Casework and the Dying Person." *Social Casework* 54 (October 1973). Also in Turner's *Differential Diagnosis and Treatment* (See entry under Deykin above.)

Gramlich, E. P. "Recognition and Management of Grief in Elderly Patients." *Geriatrics* 23 (July 1968).

Greene, Martin. "Loss of Mate—A Third Individuation Process." *Clinical Social Work Journal* (Spring 1976).

Grollman, Earl, ed. *What Helped Me—When My Loved One Died.* Boston: Beacon Press, 1981.

———. *When Your Loved One is Dying.* Boston: Beacon Press, 1980.

Group for the Advancement of Psychiatry. Report no. 12 *The Right to Die: Decision and Decision Makers.* New York: Group for the Advancement of Psychiatry, 1973.

Harper, Bernice. *Death—Coping Mechanism of the Health Professional.* Greenville, S.C.: Southeastern University Press, 1977.

Jacobson, Edith. *Depression: Comparative Studies of Normal, Neurotic, and Psychotic Conditions.* New York: International Universities Press, 1971.

Klugman, David; Litman, Robert; and Wold, Carl. "Suicide: Answering the Cry for Help." *Social Work* 10 (October 1965).

Krupp, George. "Maladaptive Reactions to the Death of a Family Member." *Social Casework* 53 (July 1972).

Kübler-Ross, Elisabeth. *On Death and Dying.* New York: Macmillan Co., 1970.

———. "The Right to Die with Dignity." *Bulletin of the Menninger Clinic* 36 (May 1972).

Lebow, Grace. "Facilitating Adaptation in Anticipatory Mourning." *Social Casework* 57 (July 1976).

LeShan, Eda. *Learning to Say Good-bye: When a Parent Dies.* New York: Avon Press, 1978.

Lindemann, Erich. "Symptomatology and Management of Acute Grief." In *Crisis Intervention: Selected Readings.* Edited by Howard Parad. New York: Family Service Association of America, 1965.

Milner, Clara. "Compassionate Care for the Dying Person." *Health and Social Work* 5 (May 1980).

Mintz, Ronald. "Basic Considerations in the Psychotherapy of the Depressed Suicidal Patient." *American Journal of Psychotherapy* 25 (January 1971).

Murray, D. C. "The Suicide Threat: Base Rates and Appropriate Therapeutic Strategy." *Psychotherapy: Theory, Research, and Practice* 9 (Summer 1972).

Nolfi, Mary. "Families in Grief: The Question of Casework Intervention." *Social Work* 12 (October 1967).

Pattison, E. Mansell. "The Experience of Dying." *American Journal of Psychotherapy* 21 (January 1967).

Pilsecker, Carleton. "Help for the Dying." *Social Work* 20 (May 1975).

Rosen, Helen, and Cohen, Harriette. "Children's Reactions to Sibling Loss." *Clinical Social Work Journal* 9 (Fall 1981).

Scher, Jordan. "The Depessions and Structure: An Existential Approach to Their Understanding and Treatment." *American Journal of Psychotherapy* 25 (July 1971).

Schneidman, E., and Farberow, N., eds. *Clues to Suicide.* New York: McGraw Hill, 1957. See especially Bennett, A. E. "Suggestions for Suicide Prevention."

Schoenberg, B.; Carr, A.; and Perets, D., eds. *Loss and Grief.* New York and London: Columbia University Press, 1970. See especially "Object Loss and Somatic Symptoms."

Simos, Bertha. "Grief Therapy to Facilitate Healthy Restitution." *Social Casework* 58 (June 1977).

Stone, Alan, and Shein, Harvey. "Psychotherapy of the Hospital Suicidal Patient." *American Journal of Psychotherapy* 22 (January 1968).

Stuart, Richard. "Casework Treatment of Depression Viewed as an Interpersonal Disturbance." *Social Work* 12 (April 1967).

Tull, Anne. "The Stresses of Clinical Social Work With the Terminally Ill." *Smith College Studies in Social Work* 45 (February 1975).

Walzer, Hank. "Casework Treatment of the Depressed Parent." *Social Casework* 42 (December 1961). Also in Turner's *Differential Diagnosis and Treatment.* (See entry under Deykin above.)

Weisberg, Lillian. "Casework with the Terminally Ill." *Social Casework* 55 (June 1974).

Weisman, Avery. *On Death and Denying: A Psychiatric Study of Terminality*. New York: Behavioral Publications, 1972.

Weissman, Myrna. "Casework and Pharmacotherapy in Treatment of Depression." *Social Casework* 53 (January 1972).

_____, and Siegel, R. "The Depressed Woman and Her Rebellious Adolescent." *Social Casework* 53 (November 1972).

Wenz, Friedrich. "Family Constellation Factors, Depression, and Parent Suicide Potential," *American Journal of Orthopsychiatry* 49 (January 1979).

Wetzel, Janice, and Redmond, Franklin. "A Person-Environment Study of Depression." *Social Service Review* 54 (September 1980).

e. Borderline States

Adler, Gerald. "The Myth of the Alliance with Borderline Patients." *American Journal of Psychiatry* 136 (May 1978).

Blanck, Rubin. "Countertransference in Treatment of the Borderline Patient." *Clinical Social Work Journal* (Summer 1973).

Bintzler, Janet. "Diagnosis and Treatment of Borderline Personality Organization." *Clinical Social Work Journal* 6 (Summer 1978).

Briggs, Dean. "The Trainee and the Borderline Client: Countertransference Pitfalls." *Clinical Social Work Journal* 7 (Summer 1979).

Carrilio, Terry. "Testing a Theory of the Borderline-Narcissistic Personality." *Social Work* 26 (March 1981).

Colt, Ann. "Casework Treatment of a Borderline Client." *Social Casework* 48 (October 1967).

Chessick, Richard. "The 'Crucial Dilemma' of the Therapist in the Psychotherapy of Borderline Patients." *American Journal of Psychotherapy* 22 (October 1968).

_____. "The Psychotherapy of Borderline Patients." *American Journal of Psychotherapy* 20 (July 1966).

Edward, Joyce; Ruskin, Nathene; and Turrini, Patsy. *Separation—Individuation: Theory and Clinical Practice*. New York: Gardner Press Series in Clinical Social Work, 1981.

Farber, Laura. "Casework Treatment of Ambulatory Schizophrenics." *Social Casework* 39 (January 1958).

Freed, Anne. "The Borderline Personality," *Social Casework* 61 (November 1980).

Geleerd, Elisabeth. "Borderline States in Childhood and Adolescence." *Psychoanalytic Study of the Child* 13 (1958).

Grinker, Roy; Werble, Beatrice; and Drye, Robert. *The Borderline Syndrome*. New York: Basic Books, 1968.

Gunderson, John, and Singer, Margaret. "Defining Borderline Patients: An Overview." *American Journal of Psychiatry* 132 (January 1975).

Harticollis, Peter, ed. *Borderline Personality Disorders*. New York: International Universities Press, 1977.

Kaufman, Irving. "Therapeutic Considerations of Borderline Personality Structure." In *Ego Psychology and Dynamic Casework: Papers from the Smith College for Social Work*. Edited by Howard Parad. New York: Family Service Association of America, 1958.

Kernberg, Otto. *Borderline Conditions and Pathological Narcissism*. New York: Jason Aronson, 1975.

_____. "Borderline Personality Organization." *Journal of the American Psychoanalytic Asociation* 15 (July 1967).

Kohut, Heinz. *The Restoration of Self*. New York: International Universities Press, 1977.

Lackie, Bruce. "Mahler Applied." *Clinical Social Work Journal* 3 (Spring 1975).

Mahler, Margaret. "A Study of the Separation—Individuation Process and Its Possible Application to Borderline Phenomena in the Psychoanalytic Situation." *Psychoanalytic Study of the Child* 28 (1973).

Masterson, James. *New Perspectives on the Psychotherapy of the Borderline Adult*. New York: Brunner/Mazel, 1978.

_____. *Psychotherapy of the Borderline Adult: A Developmental Approach*. New York: Brunner/Mazel, 1976.

Oberman, Edna. "The Use of Time-Limited Relationship Therapy with Borderline Patients." *Smith College Studies in Social Work* 37 (February 1967).

Rosenfeld, Sara, and Spruce, Marjorie. "An Attempt to Formulate the Meaning of the Concept Borderline." *Psychoanalytic Study of the Child* 18 (1963).

Schmideberg, Melitta. "The Borderline Personality." In *The American Handbook of Psychiatry*. Edited by Silvano Arieti New York: Basic Books, 1959.

Shapiro, Edward. "The Psychodynamic and Developmental Psychology of the Borderline Patient: A Review of the Literature." *American Journal of Psychiatry* 135 (November 1978).

Siporin, Max. "Deviant Behavior Theory in Social Work: Diagnosis and Treatment." *Social Work* 10 (July 1965).
Stuart, Richard. "Supportive Casework with Borderline Patients." *Social Work* 9 (January 1964). Also in *Differential Diagnosis and Treatment in Social Work*. Edited by Francis Turner. New York: The Free Press, 1968, and 2d ed., 1976.
Taylor, Shirley, and Siegel, Norma. "Treating the Separation-Individuation Conflict." *Social Casework* 59 (June 1978).
Weinberger, Jerome. "Basic Concepts in Diagnosis and Treatment of Borderline States." In Parad's *Ego Psychology and Dynamic Casework*. (See entry under Kaufman above.)
Zetzel, Elizabeth. "A Developmental Approach to the Borderline Patient." *The American Journal of Psychiatry* 128 (January 1971).

f. Clinical Diagnoses with Children and Adolescents
Cohen, D., and Caparulo, B. "Childhood Autism." *Children Today* 4 (July-August 1975).
French, Alfred. *Disturbed Children and Their Families: Innovations in Evaluation and Treatment*. 2d ed., rev. New York: Human Sciences Press, 1979.
Grossberg, Sidney, and Crandall, Louise. "Father Loss and Father Absences in Preschool Children." *Clinical Social Work Journal* 6 (Summer, 1978).
Group for the Advancement of Psychiatry. Report no. 87. *From Diagnosis to Treatment: An Approach to Treatment Planning for the Emotionally Disturbed Child*. New York: Mental Health Materials Center, 1973.
————. Report no. 62. *Psychopathological Disorders in Childhood: Theoretical Considerations and a Proposed Classification*. New York: Group for the Advancement of Psychiatry, 1966.
Hobbs, Nicholas, ed. *Issues in the Classification of Children: A Sourcebook on Categories, Labels, and Their Consequences*. 2 vols. San Francisco: Jossey-Bass, 1974.
————; Egerton, J.; and Matheny, M. "Classifying Children." *Children Today* 4 (July/August 1975).
King, Peter. "Early Infantile Autism: Relation to Schizophrenia." *Journal of the American Academy of Child Psychiatry* 14 (Autumn 1975).

Kupfer, David; Detre, Thomas; and Koral, Jacqueline. "Relationship of Certain Childhood 'Traits' to Adult Psychiatric Disorders." *American Journal of Orthopsychiatry* 45 (January 1975).

Lewis, Dorothy, and Balla, David. "Sociopathy and Its Synonyms: Inappropriate Diagnosis in Child Psychiatry." *American Journal of Psychiatry* 132 (July 1975).

Massie, Henry. "The Early Natural History of Childhood Psychosis." *Journal of the American Academy of Child Psychiatry* 14 (Autumn 1975).

Murphy, Lois. "Problems in Recognizing Emotional Disturbance in Children." *Child Welfare 42 (December 1963).*

Oakland, Thomas, and Beeman, Phillips. "Assessing Minority Group Children." Special Issue of the *Journal of School Psychology*. New York: Behavioral Publications, 1973.

Pine, Fred. "On the Concept 'Borderline' in Children: A Clinical Essay." *Psychoanalytic Study of the Child* (1974).

Stone, Cynthia, and Bernstein, Laura. "Case Management With Borderline Children: Theory and Practice." *Clinical Social Work Journal* 8 (Fall 1980).

Roberts, Maria. "Reciprocal Nature of Parent-Infant Interaction: Implications for Child Maltreatment." *Child Welfare* 58 (June 1979).

G. DIFFERENTIAL INTERVENTION (TREATMENT)

1. GENERAL PRINCIPLES

Atherton, Charles; Mitchell, Sandra; and Schein, E. B. "Locating Points for Intervention." *Social Casework* 54 (March 1971).

Bandler, Louise. "Casework: A Process of Socialization: Gains, Limitations, Conclusions." In *The Drifters*. Edited by Eleanor Pavenstedt. Boston: Little, Brown and Co., 1967.

Bloom Mary. "Usefulness of the Home Visit for Diagnosis and Treatment." *Social Casework* 54 (February 1973).

Eggleston, Sarah. "Supportive Casework: Its Theoretical and Practical Meaning to Caseworkers." *Smith College Studies in Social Work* 38 (June 1968).

Ewalt, Patricia, and Kutz, Janice. "An Examination of Advice Giving as a Therapeutic Intervention." *Smith College Studies in Social Work* 47 (November 1976).

Fantz, Berta. "Integrating Social and Psychological Theories in Social Work Practice." *Smith College Studies in Social Work* 34 (June 1964).

Fleshman, Bob, and Fryrear, Jerry. *The Arts in Therapy*. Chicago: Nelson-Hall, 1981.

Gelfand, Bernard. "Emerging Trends in Social Treatment." *Social Casework* 53 (March 1972).

Greene, Mary, and Orman, Betty. "Nurturing the Unnurtured." *Social Casework* 62 (September 1981).

Grinnell, Richard, Jr. "Environmental Modification: Casework's Concern or Casework's Neglect?" *Social Service Review* 47 (June 1973).

Grumet, Gerald. "Telephone Therapy: A Review and Case Report." *American Journal of Orthopsychiatry* 49 (October 1979).

Jayaratne, Srinika. "A Study of Clinical Eclecticism." *Social Service Review* 52 (December 1978).

Mullen, Edward. "The Relation Between Diagnosis and Treatment in Casework." *Social Casework* 50 (April 1969).

Nelsen, Judith. "Support: A Necessary Condition for Change." *Social Work* 25 (September 1980).

Polansky, Norman. "Help for the Helpless." *Smith College Studies in Social Work* 49 (June 1979).

Prosky, Phoebe. "Family Therapy: An Orientation." *Clinical Social Work Journal* 2 (Spring 1974).

Rauch, Julia. "Gender as a Factor in Practice." *Social Work* 23 (September 1978).

Reid, William, and Shapiro, Barbara. "Client Reactions to Advice." *Social Service Review* 43 (June 1969).

Selby, Lola. "Support Revisited." *Social Service Review* 53 (December 1979).

Siporin, Max. "Situational Assessment and Intervention." *Social Casework* 53 (February 1972).

―――――. "Social Treatment: A New-Old Helping Method." *Social Work* 15 (July 1970).

Strean, Herbert. "Choosing Among Practice Modalities." *Clinical Social Work Journal* 2 (Spring 1974).

———, et al. "A Critique of Some of the Newer Treatment Modalities." *Clinical Social Work Journal* 9 (Fall 1981).
Turner, Francis J., ed. *Differential Diganosis and Treatment in Social Work*. New York: The Free Press, 1968, 2d ed. 1976.
Whittaker, James. *Social Treatment: An Approach to Interpersonal Helping*. Aldine Publishing, 1974.

2. OUTREACH

Ambrosino, Salvatore. "A Family Agency Reaches Out to a Slum Ghetto." *Social Work* 11 (October, 1966).
Bloom, Mary. "Usefulness of the Home Visit for Diagnosis and Treatment." *Social Casework* 54 (February 1973).
Chaskel, Ruth. "Assertive Casework in a Short-term Situation." In *Crisis Intervention: Selected Readings*. Edited by Howard Parad. New York: Family Service Association of America, 1965.
Children Today 4 (May-June 1975). Entire issue on outreach, child abuse, etc.
Cowan, Barbara, et al. "Holding Unwilling Clients in Treatment." *Social Casework* 50 (March 1969).
Faucett, Emily. "A Re-Evaluation of the Home Visit in Casework Practice." *Social Casework* 42 (November 1961).
Haas, Walter. "Reaching Out—A Dynamic Concept in Casework." *Social Work* 4 (July 1959).
Herre, Ernest. "Aggressive Casework in a Protective Services Unit." *Social Casework* 46 (June 1965).
Jacobucci, Louis. "Casework Treatment of the Neglectful Mother." *Social Casework* 46 (April 1965).
Levine, Rachel. "Treatment in the Home: An Experiment with Low Income Multi-Problem Families." *Social Work* 9 (January 1964).
MacGarrity, Michael. "Bulding Early Relationships in Schools of Social Work." *Social Casework* 56 (June 1975).
McKinney, Geraldine. "Adapting Family Therapy to Multideficit Families." *Social Casework* (June 1970).
Maluccio, Anthony. "Action as a Tool in Casework Practice." *Social Casework* 55 (January 1974).
Nichols, Beverly. "The Abused Wife Problem." *Social Casework* 57 (January 1976).

Orcutt, Ben. "Casework Intervention and the Problems of the Poor."
Social Casework 54 (February 1973).

Overtòn, Alice. "Serving Families Who Don't Want Help." *Social
Casework* 34 (July 1953).

Sackin, David, and Raffe, Irving. "Multi-problem Families: A
Social-Psychological Perspective: Sometimes I Feel Like a
Motherless Child." *Clinical Social Work Journal* 4 (Spring 1976).

Schroeder, Christine. "Communicating With Hard to Reach
Patients." *Health and Social Work* 5 (February 1980).

Shorkey, Clayton. "A Review of Methods Used in the Treatment of
Abusing Parents." *Social Casework* 60 (June 1979).

Sunley, Robert. "New Dimensions in Reaching-Out Casework."
Social Work 13 (April 1968).

Toseland, Ron. "Increasing Access: Outreach Methods in Social Work
Practice." *Social Casework* 62 (April 1981).

3. SHORT-TERM INTERVENTION

Bauer, Roger, and Stein, Joan. "Sex Counseling on Campus:
Short-Term Treatment Techniques." *American Journal of
Orthopsychiatry* 43 (October 1973).

Blinzinsky, Martin, and Reid, William. "Problem Focus and Change
in a Brief Treatment Model." *Social Work* 25 (March 1980).

Ewalt, Patricia. "The Case for Immediate Brief Intervention." *Social
Work* 21 (January 1976).

Goldmeier, John. "Short-Term Models in Long-Term Treatment."
Social Work 21 (September 1976).

Kerns, Elizabeth. "Planned Short-Term Treatment, A New Service
to Adolescents," *Social Casework* 51 (June 1970).

Kogan, Leonard. "The Short-Term Case in a Family Agency: Part I.
The Study Plan." *Social Casework* 38 (May 1957).

_____. "The Short-Term Case in a Family Agency: Part II. Results
of Study." *Social Casework* 38 (June 1957).

_____. "The Short-Term Case in a Family Agency: Part III. Further
Results and Conclusions." *Social Casework* 38 (July 1957).

Lantz, James, and Werk, Kay. "Short-Term Casework: A Rational
Emotive Approach." *Child Welfare* 55 (January 1976).

Laughlin, John, and Bressler, Robert. "A Family Agency Problem for Heavily Indebted Families." *Social Casework* 52 (December 1971).

Lemon, Elizabeth, and Goldstein, Shirley. "The Use of Time Limits in Planned Brief Casework." *Social Casework* 59 (December 1978).

Leventhal, Theodore, and Weisberger, Gerald. "An Evaluation of a Large-Scale Brief Therapy Program for Children." *American Journal of Orthopsychiatry* 45 (January 1975).

Nebl, Nikolaus. "Essential Elements in Short-Term Treatment." *Social Casework* 52 (June 1971).

Norman, Jennie. "Short-Term Treatment with the Adolescent Client." *Social Casework* 61 (February 1980).

Oberman, Edna. "The Use of Time Limited Relationship Therapy with Borderline Patients." *Smith College Studies in Social Work* 37 (February 1967).

Oxley, Genevieve. "Short-Term Therapy with Student Couples." *Social Casework* 54 (April 1973).

Parad, Libbie. "Short-Term Treatment: An Overview of Historical Trends, Issues and Potentials." *Smith College Studies in Social Work* 41 (February 1971).

Plouffe, Patricia. "The Use of Brief Psychoanalytically Oriented Psychotherapy by Clinical Social Workers." *Smith College Studies in Social Work* 50 (June 1980).

Rabiner, Edwin; Wells, Carl; and Yager, Joel. "A Model for Brief Hospital Treatment of the Disadvantaged Psychiatrically Ill." *American Journal of Orthopsychiatry* 43 (October 1973).

Reid, William. *The Task-Centered System.* New York: Columbia University Press, 1978.

―――. "Test of Task-Centered Approach." *Social Work* 20 (January 1975).

―――, and Epstein, Laura. *Task-Centered Casework.* New York: Columbia University Press, 1972.

―――, eds. *Task-Centered Practice.* New York: Columbia University Press, 1977.

―――; and Shyne, Ann. *Brief and Extended Casework.* New York: Columbia University Press, 1969.

Rosenberg, Blanca. "Planned Short-Term Treatment in Developmental Crises." *Social Casework* 56 (April 1975).

Strean, Herbert, and Blatt, A. "Long or Short-Term Therapy?" *Journal of Contemporary Psychotherapy* 1 (Winter 1969).

Wattie, Brenda. "Evaluating Short-Term Casework in a Family Agency." *Social Casework* 54 (December 1973).

4. CRISIS INTERVENTION

Baldwin, Bruce. "Crisis Intervention in Professional Practice: Implications for Clinical Training." *American Journal of Orthopsychiatry* 47 (October 1977).

Bergman, Anne. "Emergency Room: A Role for Social Workers." *Health and Social Work* 1 (February 1976).

Birnbaum, Freda; Coplon, Jennifer; and Scharff, Irene. "Crisis Intervention After a Natural Disaster." *Social Casework* 54 (November 1973).

Bonnefil, Margaret, and Jacobson, Gerald. "Family Crisis Intervention." *Clinical Social Work Journal* 7 (Fall 1979).

Brown, H. Frederick. "Crisis Intervention Treatment in Child Abuse Programs." *Social Casework* 60 (July 1979).

Clifford, Glen, and Odin, Katharine. "Young Adulthood: A Developmental Phase." *Smith College Studies in Social Work* 44 (February 1974).

Ewalt, Patricia "The Crisis Treatment Approach in a Child Guidance Clinic." *Social Casework* 54 (July 1973).

Farberow, Norman et al. "Suicide Prevention Around the Clock." *American Journal of Orthopsychiatry* 36 (April 1966).

Feld, Allen. "Reflections of the Agnes Flood." *Social Work* 18 (September 1973)

Fox, Sandra, and Scherl, Donald. "Crisis Intervention with Victims of Rape." *Social Work* 17 (January 1972).

Golan, Naomi. "Crisis Theory." In *Social Work Treatment: Interlocking Theoretical Approaches*. Edited by Francis Turner. New York: The Free Press, 1974.

————. "Intervention at Times of Transition." *Social Casework* 61 (May 1980).

————. *Treatment in Crisis Situations*. New York: The Free Press, 1978.

————. "Short-Term Crisis Intervention: An Approach to Serving Children and Their Families." *Child Welfare* 50 (February 1971).

————. "When Is a Client in Crisis?" *Social Casework* 50 (July 1969).

Goldberg, Stanley. "Family Tasks and Reactions in the Crisis of Death." *Social Casework* 54 (July 1973).

Grumet, Gerald, and Trachtman, David. "Psychiatric Social Workers in the Emergency Department." *Health and Social Work* 1 (August 1976).

Henderson, Howard. "Helping Families in Crises: Police and Social Work Intervention." *Social Work* 21 (July 1976).

Hoffman, David, and Remmel, Mary. "Uncovering the Precipitant in Crisis Intervention." *Social Casework* 56 (May 1975).

Lindemann, Erich. "Symptomatology and Management of Acute Grief." *Crisis Intervention: Selected Readings*. Edited by Howard Parad. New York: Family Service Association of America, 1965.

McCombie, Sharon. "Characteristics of Rape Victims Seen in Crisis Intervention." *Smith College Studies in Social Work* 46 (March 1976).

Parad, Howard, ed. *Crisis Intervention: Selected Readings*. New York: Family Service Association of America, 1965.

Puryear, Douglas. *Helping People in Crisis: A Practical, Family Oriented Approach to Effective Crisis Intervention*. San Francisco: Jossey-Bass, 1979.

Rapoport, Lydia. "Crisis Intervention as a Mode of Brief Treatment." In *Theories of Social Casework*. Edited by Robert Roberts and Robert Nee. Chicago: University of Chicago Press, 1970.

_____. "The State of Crisis: Some Theoretical Considerations." *Social Service Review* 36 (March 1962). Also in Parad's *Crisis Intervention*.

_____. "Working with Families in Crisis: An Exploration in Preventive Intervention." *Social Work* 7 (July 1962). Also in Parad's *Crisis Intervention*.

Rapoport, Rhona. "Normal Crisis, Family Structure and Mental Health." *Family Process* 2 (January 1963). Also in Parad's *Crisis Intervention*.

Rice, Elizabeth, and Krakow, Sylvia. "Hospitalization of a Parent for Mental Illness: A Crisis for Children." *American Journal of Orthopsychiatry* 36 (October 1966).

Scherz, Frances. "Maturational Crises and Parent-Child Interaction." *Social Casework* 52 (June 1971).

Singer, Ann. "A Program for Young Mothers and Their Babies." *Social Casework* 52 (November 1971).

Smith, Larry. "Crisis Intervention in Practice." *Social Casework* 60 (February 1979).
_____. "A General Model of Crisis Intervention." *Clinical Social Work Journal* 4 (Fall 1976).
_____. "A Review of Crisis Intervention Theory." *Social Casework* 59 (July 1978).
Strickler, Martin. "Applying Crisis Theory in a Community Clinic." *Social Casework* 46 (March 1965).
_____. "Crisis Intervention and the Climacteric Man." *Social Casework* 56 (February 1975).
_____, and Bonnefil, Margaret. "Crisis Intervention and Social Casework: Similarities and Differences in Problem Solving." *Clinical Social Work Journal* 2 (Spring 1974).
Walton, Maxine; Reeves, Gloria; and Shannon, Robert. "Crisis Team Intervention in School Community Unrest." *Social Casework* 52 (January 1971).
Wiseman, Reva. "Crisis Theory: The Process of Divorce." *Social Casework* 56 (April 1975).

5. FAMILY TREATMENT

See related items under Family Assessment

Ackerman, Nathan. *Treating the Troubled Family*. New York: Basic Books, 1966.
Anderson, Linda et al. "Training in Family Treatment: Needs and Objectives." *Social Casework* 60 (June 1979).
Bardill, Donald, and Bevliacqua, Joseph. "Family Interviewing by Two Caseworkers." *Social Casework* 45 (May 1964).
Bell, John. "Contrasting Approaches in Marital Counseling." *Family Process* 6 (March 1967).
Bloch, Donald. *Techniques of Family Psychotherapy*. New York: Grune and Stratton, 1973.
Bowen, Murray. *Family Therapy in Clinical Practice*. New York: Jason Aronson, 1978.
Butehorn, Loretta. "A Plan for Identifying Priorities in Treating Multi-Problem Families." *Child Welfare* 57 (June 1978).
Cohn, Ann. "Effective Treatment of Child Abuse and Neglect." *Social Work* 24 (November 1979).

Couch, Elizabeth. *Joint and Family Interviews in the Treatment of Marital Problems*. New York: Family Service Association of America, 1969.

Ehrenkranz, Shirley. "A Study of Joint Interviewing in the Treatment of Marital Problems: Part I." *Social Casework* 48 (October 1967).

――――. "A Study of Joint Interviewing in the Treatment of Marital Problems: Part II." *Social Casework* 48 (November 1967).

Elbow, Margaret, ed. *Patterns in Family Violence: Social Casework Reprint Series*. New York: Family Service Association of America, 1980.

Foley, Vincent. *An Introduction to Family Therapy*. New York: Grune and Stratton, 1974.

Fontane, Arlene. "Using Family of Origin Material in Short-Term Marriage Counseling." *Social Casework* 60 (November 1979).

Geist, Joanne, and Gerber, N. "Joint Interviewing: A Treatment Technique with Marital Partners." *Social Casework* 41 (February 1960). Also in *Differential Diagnosis and Treatment in Social Work*. Edited by Francis Turner. New York: The Free Press, 1968, 2d ed. 1976.

Goldberg, Stanley. "Family Tasks and Reactions in the Crisis of Death." *Social Casework* 54 (July 1973).

Goldmeier, John. "Intervention in the Continuum from Divorce to Family Reconstitution." *Social Casework* 61 (January 1980).

Guerin, Philip, Jr., ed. *Family Therapy: Theory and Practice*. New York: Gardner Press, 1976.

Haley, Jay. *Problem Solving Therapy: New Strategies for Effective Family Therapy*. San Francisco: Jossey Bass, 1978.

Harris, Oliver, and Janzen, Curtis, eds. *Family Treatment in Social Work Practice*. Itasca, Ill., F.E. Peacock, 1980.

Jones, Mary Ann; Magura, Stephen; and Shyne, Ann. "Effective Practice with Families in Protective and Preventive Services: What Works?" *Child Welfare* 60 (February 1981).

Jones, Susan. *Family Therapy: A Comparison of Approaches*. Bowie, Md.: Robert J. Brady Co., 1980.

Kantor, David, and Lehr, Williams. *Inside the Family*. San Francisco: Jossey-Bass, 1975.

King, Charles. "Family Therapy with the Deprived Family." *Social Casework* 48 (April 1967).

Langsley, Donald, and Kaplan, D. *The Treatment of Families in Crisis*. New York: Grune and Stratton, 1969.

Leader, Arthur. "The Notion of Responsibility in Family Therapy." *Social Casework* 60 (March 1979).

Letulle, Leslie. "Family Therapy in Residential Treatment for Children." *Social Work* 24 (January 1979).

The Many Dimensions of Family Practice: Proceedings of the North American Symposium on Family Practice. New York: Family Service Association of America, 1980.

Minuchin, Salvador. *Families and Family Treatment.* Cambridge, Mass.: Harvard University Press, 1975.

Mostwin, Danuta. *Social Dimension of Family Treatment.* Washington, D.C.: National Association of Social Workers, 1980.

Moultrup, David. "Towards an Integrated Model of Family Therapy." *Clinical Social Work Journal* 9 (Summer 1981).

Orcutt, Ben. "Family Treatment of Poverty Level families." *Social Casework* 58 (February 1977).

Ostbloom, Norman, and Crase, Sedahlia. "A Model for Conceptualizing Child Abuse Causation and Intervention." *Social Casework* 61 (March 1980).

Prosky, Phoebe. "Family Therapy: An Orientation." *Clinical Social Work Journal* 2 (Spring 1974).

Ranieri, Ralph, and Pratt, Theodore. "Sibling Therapy." *Social Work* 23 (September 1978).

Rapoport, Lydia. "Working with Families in Crises: An Exploration in Preventive Intervention." *Social Casework* 43 (July 1962).

Russell, Axel. "Limitations of Family Therapy." *Clinical Social Work Journal* 4 (Summer 1976).

Sager, Clifford, and Kaplan, H. *Progress in Group and Family Therapy.* New York: Brunner/Mazel, 1973.

Satir, Virginia. *Conjoint Family Therapy.* Palo Alto, Calif.: Science and Behavior Books, 1964.

Scherz, Frances. "Family Treatment Concepts." *Social Casework* 49 (April 1968).

_____. "Theory and Practice in Family Therapy." In *Theories of Social Casework.* Edited by Robert Roberts and Robert Nee. Chicago: University of Chicago Press, 1970.

Schilling, Susan, and Gross, Ellen. "Stages of Family Therapy: A Developmental Model." *Cinical Social Work Journal* 7 (Summer 1979).

Schulman, Gerda. "Teaching Family Therapy to Social Work Students." *Social Casework* 57 (July 1976).

Segal, Robert. "Integrating Art Form Therapies and Family Therapy." *Social Casework* 62 (April 1981).
Sherman, Sanford. "Intergenerative Discontinuity and Therapy of the Family." *Social Casework* 48 (April 1967).
Sholtis, Helen. "The Management of Marital Counseling Cases." *Social Casework* 45 (February 1964). Also in Turner's *Differential Diagnosis and Treatment.* (See entry under Geist above.)
Shorkey, Clayton. "A Review of Methods Used in the Treatment of Abusing Parents." *Social Casework* 60 (January 1979).
Sigal, John et al. "Problems in Measuring the Success of Family Therapy in a Common Clinical Setting: Impasse and Solutions." *Family Process* 15 (June 1976).
Siporin, Max. "Marriage and Family Therapy in Social Work." *Social Casework* 61 (January 1980).
_____. "Teaching Family and Marriage Therapy." *Social Casework* 62 (January 1981).
Wagner, Nathaniel, and Harris, Gloria. "Treatment of Sexual Dysfunction and Casework Techniques." *Clinical Social Work Journal* 1 (Winter 1973).
Wald, Esther. *The Remarried Family: Challenge and Promise.* New York: Family Service Association of America, 1981.
Wallerstein, Judith, and Kelly, Joan. *Surviving the Breakup.* New York: Basic Books, 1980.
Wells, Susan. "A Model of Therapy with Abusive and Neglectful Families." *Social Work* 26 (March 1981).
Williams, Frank. "Family Therapy: A Critical Assessment." *American Journal of Orthopsychiatry* 37 (October 1967).
Wiseman, Reva. "Crisis Theory and the Process of Divorce." *Social Casework* 56 (April 1975).

H. TERMINATION AND TRANSFER

Appelberg, Esther. "The Dependent Child and the Changing Worker." *Child Welfare* 48 (July 1969).
Barish, Samoan. "On Interruptions in Treatment." *Clinical Social Work Journal* 8 (Spring 1980).
Bolen, Jane. "Easing the Pain of Termination for Adolescents." *Social Casework* 53 (November 1972).

Brown, Selma. "Time, Content and Worker as Factors in Discontinuity." *Smith College Studies in Social Work* 39 (June 1969).

Bywaters, Paul. "Ending Casework Relationships." *Social Work Today* 6 (August 1975).

Dillon, Carolyn. "A Study of Goal Formulation and Implementation." *Smith College Studies in Social Work* 38 (June 1968).

Flesch, Regina. *Treatment Considerations in the Reassignment of Clients*. New York: Family Service Association of America, 1947.

Fox, Evelyn; Nelson, Marion; and Bolman, William. "The Termination Process: A Neglected Dimension in Social Work." *Social Work* 14 (October 1969).

Fugeri, Lena. "The Futility of Child Therapy." *Clinical Social Work Journal* 4 (Spring 1976).

Gould, Robert. "Students' Experience with the Termination Phase of Individual Treatment." *Smith College Studies in Social Work* 48 (June 1978).

Hannigan, Kathleen. "Post Treatment Integration of Psychotherapeutic Influence." *Smith College Studies in Social Work* 45 (June 1975).

Hiatt, Harold. "The Problem of Termination of Psychotherapy." *American Journal of Psychotherapy* 19 (October 1965).

Hollis, Florence. "Continuance and Discontinuance in Marital Counseling and Some Observations on Joint Interviews." *Social Casework* 49 (March 1968).

Husband, Diane, and Schuenemann, Henry. "The Use of Group Process in Teaching Termination." *Child Welfare* 51 (October 1972).

Kadushin, Alfred. *The Social Work Interview*. New York: Columbia University Press, 1973.

Levinson, Hilliard. "Termination of Psychotherapy: Some Salient Issues." *Social Casework* 58 (October 1977).

Mayer, John, and Rosenblatt, Aaron. "Client Disengagement and Alternative Treatment Resources." *Social Casework* 47 (January 1966).

Moss, Sidney, and Moss, Miriam. "When a Caseworker Leaves an Agency: The Impact on Worker and Client." *Social Casework* 48 (July 1967).

Pumpian-Mindlin, Eugene. "Comments on Techniques of Termination and Transfer in a Clinic Setting." *American Journal of Psychotherapy* 12 (July 1958).

Ripple, Lillian. "Factors Associated with Continuance in Casework Service." *Social Work* 2 (January 1957).

Ross, Alan. "Interruptions and Termination of Treatment." In *Child Psychotherapy*. Edited by Mary Haworth. New York: Basic Books, 64.

Rubin, Gerald. "Termination of Casework: The Student, Client and Field Instructor." *Journal of Education for Social Work* 4 (Spring 1968).

Sarnoff, Charles. *Latency*. New York: Jason Aronson, 1976. Chap. 6. "Terminating Psychotherapy with a Child in the Latency Stage."

Shafer, Roy. "Termination in Brief Psychotherapy." *International Journal of Psychoanalytic Psychotherapy* 2 (May 1973).

Shapiro, Constance. "Termination: A Neglected Concept in the Social Work Curriculum." *Journal of Education for Social Work* 16 (Spring 1980).

Weddington, William, and Cavenar, Jesse. "Termination Initiated by the Therapist: A Countertransference Storm." *American Journal of Psychiatry* 136 (October 1979).

I. USE OF SUPERVISION AND CONSULTATION

Abramczyk, Lois. "The New M.S.W. Supervisor: Problems of Role Transition." *Social Casework* 61 (February 1980).

Akin, Gib, and Weil, Marie. "The Prior-Question: How do Supervisors Learn to Supervise?" *Social Casework* 62 (October 1981).

Apaka, Tsuneko; Hirsh, Sidney; and Kleidman, Sylvia. "Establishing Group Supervision in a Hospital Social Work Department." *Social Work* 12 (October 1967).

Arndt, Hilda. "Effective Supervision in a Public Welfare Setting." *Public Welfare* 31 (Summer 1973).

Austin, Michael. *Supervisory Management for the Human Services*. Englewood Cliffs, N.J.: Prentice-Hall, 1981. ,

Bruck, Max. "The Relationship Between Student Anxiety, Self-Awareness, and Self-Concept and Student Competence in Casework." *Social Casework* 44 (March 1963).

Caplan, Gerald. *The Theory and Practice of Mental Health Consultation*. New York: Basic Books, 1970.

Carter, Bryan. "School Mental Health Consultation: A Clinical Social Work Interventive Technique." *Clinical Social Work Journal* 3 (Fall 1975).

Davis, Donald. "Teaching and Administrative Functions in Supervision." *Social Work* 10 (April 1965).

Fox, Raymond. "Supervision by Contract." *Social Casework* 55 (April 1974).

Gizynski, Martha. "Self Awareness of the Supervisor in Supervision." *Clinical Social Work Journal* 6 (Fall 1978).

Green, Rose. "The Consultant and the Consultation Process." *Child Welfare* 44 (October 1965).

Group for the Advancement of Psychiatry. Report no. 104. *Psychiatric Consultation in Mental Retardation*. New York: Group for the Advancement of Psychiatry, 1979.

Hawthorne, Lillian. "Games Supervisors Play." *Social Work* 20 (May 1975).

Kadushin, Alfred. "Games People Play in Supervision." *Social Work* 13 (July 1968).

_____. *Supervision in Social Work*. New York: Columbia University Press, 1976.

_____. "Supervisor-Supervisee: A Survey." *Social Work* 19 (May 1974).

_____, and Buckman, Miles. "Practice of Social Work Consultation: A Survey." *Social Work* 23 (September 1978).

Kahn, Eva. "The Parallel Process in Social Work Treatment and Supervision." *Social Casework* 60 (November 1978).

Kaslow, Florence et al. *Issues in Human Services*. San Francisco: Jossey-Bass, 1972.

_____. *Supervision, Consultation, and Staff Training in the Helping Professions*. San Francisco: Jossey-Bass, 1977.

Knoll, Donald. "Psychiatric Supervision for Social Work?" *Clinical Social Work Journal* 7 (Fall 1979).

Kolevzon, Michael. "Evaluating the Supervisory Relationship in Field Placements." *Social Work* 24 (May 1979).

Leader, Arthur. "An Agency's View Toward Education for Practice." *Journal of Education for Social Work* 7 (Fall 1971).

_____. "Supervision and Consultation Through Observed Interviewing." *Social Casework* 49 (May 1968).

Levy, Charles. "Inputs versus Outputs as Criteria of Competence."
Social Work 18 (March 1973).

Mannino, F. V. et al. *The Practice of Mental Health Consultation.*
New York: Halsted Press, 1975.

Mendel, Wm. M., and Solomon, P. L., eds. *The Psychiatric
Consultation.* New York: Grune and Stratton, 1968.

Middleman, Ruth, and Rhodes, Gary. "Teaching the Practice of
Supervision." *Journal of Education for Social Work* 16 (Fall 1980).

Munson, Carlton. "Evaluation of Male and Female Supervisors."
Social Work 24 (March 1979).

————, ed. *Social Work Supervision: Classic Statements and
Critical Issues.* New York: The Free Press, 1979.

————. "Style and Structure in Supervision." *Journal of Education
for Social Work* 17 (Winter 1981).

————. "Supervising the Family Therapist." *Social Casework* 61
(March 1980).

Murdaugh, Jessica. "Student Supervision Unbound." *Social Work* 19
(March 1974).

Nelsen, Judith. "Relationship Communication in Early Field Work
Conferences." *Social Casework* 55 (April 1974).

Rapoport, Lydia, ed. *Consultation in Social Work Practice.* New
York: National Association of Social Workers, 1963. See especially
"Consultation: An Overview," Lydia Rapoport; "Some
Characteristics of Consultation," Joanne Gorman; "Consultation as
a Social Work Activity," Mary Homes Gilmore.

Roberts, Robert. "Some Impressions of Mental Health Consultation
in a Poverty Area." *Social Casework* 49 (June 1968).

Rosenberg, Elinor, and Nitzberg, Harold. "The Clinical Social
Worker Becomes a Consultant." *Social Work in Health Care* 5
(Spring 1980).

Rosenblatt, Aaron, and Mayer, John. "Objectionable Supervisory
Styles: Students' Views." *Social Work* 20 (May 1975).

Shelmire, Marie et al. "The Use of a Consultant Psychiatrist in a
Family Service Agency." *Social Casework* 61 (November 1980).

Supervision and Staff Development. 10 articles reprinted from *Social
Casework.* New York: Family Service Association of America, 1966.

Towle, Charlotte. "The Consultation Process." *Social Service Review*
44 (June 1970).

Watson, Kenneth. "Differential Supervision." *Social Work* 18
(November 1973).

Wijnberg, Marion, and Schwartz, Mary. "Models of Student Supervision: the Apprentice, Growth, and Role Systems Models." *Journal of Education for Social Work* 13 (Fall 1977).

Williamson, Margaret. *Supervision: New Patterns and Processes.* New York: Association Press, 1961.

Williams, Martha. "The Problem Profile Technique in Consultation." *Social Work* 16 (July 1971).

J. INTER- AND INTRA-AGENCY COLLABORATION

Alperin, Richard. "Social Work Has a Problem: A Psychosocial Study." *Clinical Social Work Journal* 5 (Summer 1977).

Bandler, Bernard. "Interprofessional Collaboration in Training in Mental Health." *American Journal of Orthopsychiatry* 43 (January 1973).

Bartlett, Harriett. *Some Aspects of Social Casework in a Medical Setting.* New York: American Association of Medical Social Workers, 1958. See especially Chap. IV, "Physician, Patient and Social Worker," and, Chap. V, "Integrating Social Casework with the Medical Setting."

Bassoff, Betty, and Ludwig, Stephen. "Interdisciplinary Education for Health Care Professionals." *Health and Social Work* 4 (May 1979).

Bernstein, Barton. "Lawyer and Social Worker as an Interdisciplinary Team." *Social Casework* 61 (September 1980).

Black, Bertram, and Kase, Harold. "Inter-agency Cooperation in Rehabilitation and Mental Health." *Social Service Review* 37 (March 1963).

Bramberg, Jeanette; Cowin, Ruth; and Rice, Elizabeth. "A Health-Welfare Partnership to Improve Services to Mothers and Children." *Public Welfare* 24 (October 1966).

Carroll, Mary. "Collaboration with Social Work Clients: A Review of the Literature." *Child Welfare* 59 (July-August 1980).

Dickson, Donald. "Law in Social Work: Impact of Due Process." *Social Work* 21 (July 1976).

Frank, Lawrence. "Interprofessional Communication." *American Journal of Public Health* 51 (December 1961).

Hallowitz, David, and Van Dyke, Catherine. "The Role of the School as Part of the Treatment Program." *Child Welfare* 41 (June 1973).

Hardgrove, Grace. "An Interagency Service Network to Meet Needs of Rape Victims." *Social Casework* 57 (April 1976).

Heyman, Margaret. "Collaboration Between Doctor and Caseworker in a General Hospital." *Social Casework* 48 (May 1967).

Jones, Terry. "Some Thoughts on Coordination of Services." *Social Work* 20 (September 1975).

Kane, Rosalie. *Interprofessional Teamwork.* New York: Syracuse University School of Social Work, 1975.

————. *Training for Teamwork.* New York: Syracuse University School of Social Work, 1975.

Kotin, Joel, and Sharaf, Myron. "Intra-Staff Controversy at a State Mental Hospital: An Analysis of Ideological Issues." *Psychiatry* 30 (February 1967).

Lee, Stacey. "Interdisciplinary Teaming in Primary Care: A Process of Evolution and Revolution." *Social Work in Health Care* 5 (Spring 1980).

Lewis, Jerry. "The Organizational Structure of the Therapeutic Team." *Hospital and Community Psychiatry* 20 (July 1969).

Moynihan, Francis. "Family Service Agency Collaboration with Schools." *Social Casework* 47 (January 1966).

Ness, Claire. "The Agency, the Foster Parent and the Child: Partners in Communication." *Child Welfare* 39 (January 1960).

New, Peter Kong-Ming. "An Analysis of the Concept of Team Work." *Community Mental Health Journal* 4 (August 1968).

Rae, Grant; Quentin, A. F.; and Marcuse, Donald. "The Hazards of Teamwork." *American Journal of Orthopsychiatry* 38 (January 1968).

Resnick, David. "The Social Worker as Co-ordinator in Rejsidential Treatment." *Social Casework* 48 (May 1967).

Rushing, William. *The Psychiatric Professions: Power, Conflict and Adaptation in a Psychiatric Hospital Staff.* Chapel Hill, N.C.: University of North Carolina Press, 1964.

Scherrer, James. "How Social Workers Help Lawyers." *Social Work* 21 (July 1976).

Smith, Audrey. "The Social Worker in the Legal Aid Setting: A Study of Interprofessional Relationships." *Social Service Review* 44 (June 1970).

Stempler, Benj., and Stempler, Hani. "Extending the Client Connection: Using Homemaker-Caseworker Teams." *Social Casework* 62 (March 1981).

Stone, Nellie. "Effecting Interdisciplinary Coordination in Clinical Services to the Mentally Retarded." *American Journal of Orthopsychiatry* 40 (October 1970).
Straight, Elmer et al. "Collaboration: A Negotiated Contract." *Diseases of the Nervous System* 27 (July 1966).
Street, David. "Educators and Social Workers: Sibling Rivalry in the Inner City." *Social Service Review* 41 (June 1967).
Thomas, M. Duane, and Morrison, Thomas. "Interdisciplinary Team Communications: TA as a Tool." *Clinical Social Work Journal* 5 (Summer 1977).
Whitworth, Jay et al. "A Multidisciplinary, Hospital-Based Team for Child Abuse Cases: A 'Hands-On' Approach." *Child Welfare* 60 (April 1981).

K. INTERVIEWING

Baker, Nicholas. "Social Work Through an Interpreter." *Social Work* 26 (September 1981).
Bardith, Donald, and Bevilacqua, Joseph. "Family Interviewing by Two Caseworkers." *Social Casework* 45 (May 1964).
Case, Lois, and Lingerfelt, Neverlyn. "Name-calling: The Labelling Process in the Social Work Interview." *Social Service Review* 48 (March 1974).
Cormier, William, and Cormier, Sherilyn. *Interviewing Strategies for Helpers: A Guide to Assessment, Treatment and Evaluation.* Monterey, Calif.: Brooks/Cole, 1979.
Couch, Elizabeth. *Joint and Family Interviews in the Treatment of Marital Problems.* New York: Family Service Association of America, 1969.
Deschin, Celia. "Research Interviewing in Sensitive Subject Areas." *Social Work* 8 (April 1963).
Edinburg, Golda; Zinberg, Norman; and Kilman, Wendy. *Clinical Interviewing and Counseling.* New York: Appleton-Century-Crofts, 1975.
Faucett, Emily. "Multiple Client Interviewing: A Means of Assessing Family Processes." *Social Casework* 43 (March 1962).
Feldman, Yonata. "Listening and Understanding." *Clinical Social Work Journal* 3 (Summer 1975).

Fraiberg, Selma. "Some Aspects of Casework with Children: Part I. Understanding the Child Client." *Social Casework* 33 (November 1952).

_____. "Some Aspects of Casework with Children: Part II. Helping with Critical Situations." *Social Casework* 33 (December 1952).

Gareffa, Domenic, and Neff, Stanley. "Management of the Client's Seductive Behavior." *Smith College Studies in Social Work* 44 (February 1974).

Garrett, Annette. *Interviewing: Its Principles and Methods*, 3d ed. rev. New York: Family Service Association of America, 1982.

Geist, Joanne, and Gerber, Norman. "Joint Interviewing: A Treatment Technique with Marital Partners." Also in *Differential Diagnosis and Treatment in Social Work*. Edited by Francis Turner. New York: The Free Press, 1968, 2d ed. 1976.

Group for the Advancement of Psychiatry. Report no. 88. *Assessment of Sexual Function: A Guide to Interviewing*. New York: Mental Health Materials Center, 1973.

Hollis, Florence. "Continuance and Discontinuance in Marital Counseling and Some Observations on Joint Interviews." *Social Casework* 49 (March 1968).

_____. "A Profile of Early Interviews in Marital Counseling." *Social Casework* 49 (January 1968).

Kadushin, Alfred. *The Social Work Interview*. New York: Columbia University Press, 1972.

Krill, Donald. "Family Interviewing as an Intake Diagnostic Method." *Social Work* 13 (April 1968).

Scherz, Frances. "Exploring the Use of Family Interviews in Diagnosis." *Social Casework* 45 (April 1964).

_____. "Multiple-Client Interviewing: Treatment Implications." *Social Casework* 43 (March 1962).

Sherman, Sanford. "Aspects of Family Interviewing Critical for Staff Training and Education." *Social Service Review* 40 (September 1966).

Shubert, Margaret. *Interviewing in Social Work Practice: An Introduction*. New York: Council on Social Work Education, 1971.

Veague, Pamela. "Quasi-Courting in the Clinical Interview." *Smith College Studies in Social Work* 44 (February 1974).

Wineman, David. "The Life-Space Interview." *Social Work* 4 (January 1959).

L. RECORDING

Abel, Charles, and Johnson, H. Wayne. "Clients' Access to Records: Policy and Attitudes." *Social Work* 23 (January 1978).

Chea, Mary Wong. "Research on Recording." *Social Casework* 53 (March 1972).

Cooper, Shirley. "Hold the Hardware: The Use and Abuse of Tapes in Clinical Teaching and Learning." *American Journal of Orthopsychiatry* 45 (July 1975).

Dwyer, Margaret, and Urbanowski, Martha. "Student Process Recording: A Plea for Structure." *Social Casework* 46 (May 1965).

Feldman, Yonata. "Student's Training Needs as Reflected in Their Recorded Material." *Smith College Studies in Social Work* 27 (February 1957).

Freed, Anne "Clients' Rights and Casework Records." *Social Casework* 59 (October 1978).

Hamilton, Gordon. *Principles of Social Case Recording.* New York: Columbia University Press, 1946.

Iaccarino, Sandra. "Privileged Communication in Social Work." *Social Casework* 61 (June 1980).

Johnson, Harriette. "Integrating the Problem-Oriented Record with a Systems Approach to Case Assessment." *Journal of Education for Social Work* 14 (Fall 1978).

Kane, Rosalie. "Look to the Record." *Social Work* 19 (July 1974).

Lusby, Sarah, and Rudney, Bernice. "One Agency's Solution to the Recording Problem." *Social Casework* 54 (December 1973).

Martens, Wilma, and Holmstrup, Elizabeth. "Problem-oriented Recording." *Social Casework* 55 (November 1974).

Reid, William. "Developments on the Use of Organized Data." *Social Work* 19 (September 1974).

Schrier, Carol. "Guidelines for Record Keeping Under Privacy and Open Access Laws." *Social Work* 25 (November 1980).

Seaberg, Joseph. "Systematized Recording: A Follow-up." *Social Work* 15 (August 1970).

Timms, Noel. *Recording in Social Work.* London: Routledge and Kegan Paul, 1972.

Tuzil, Teresa. "Writing: A Problem-Solving Process." *Social Work* 23 (January 1978).

Urbanowski, Martha. "Recording to Measure Effectiveness." *Social Casework* 55 (November 1974).

Urdang, Esther. "In Defense of Process Recording." *Smith College Studies in Social Work* 50 (November 1979).

Wilczynski, Brahna. "New Life for Recording: Involving the Clients." *Social Work* 26 (July 1981).

Wilkie, Charlotte. "A Study of Distortions in Recorded Interviews." *Social Work* 8 (May 1963).

Wilson, Suanna. *Recording: Guidelines for Social Workers.* New York: The Free Press, 1980.

III. Special Populations

A. CHILDREN

See related items under Sexual Deviance.

Adams, Paul. *A Primer of Child Psychotherapy.* Boston: Little, Brown and Co., 1974.

Adler, Jack, *The Child Care Worker: Concepts, Tasks and Relatinships.* New York: Brunner/Mazel, 1976.

Appelberg, Esther. "The Dependent Child and the Changing Worker." *Child Welfare* 48 (July 1969).

Barnes, Marion. "Casework with Children." *Smith College Studies in Social Work* 35 (June 1965).

Burns, Brenda. "The Use of Play Techniques in the Treatment of Children." *Child Welfare* 49 (January 1970).

Carbino, Rosemarie. *Foster Parenting: An Updated Review of the Literature.* New York: Child Welfare League of America, 1980.

Chethik, Morton. "The Emotional 'Wear and Tear' of Child Therapy." *Smith College Studies in Social Work* 39 (February 1969).

Child Study Association. *What to Tell Your Child About Sex.* New York: Jason Aronson, 1974.

Cooper, Shirley, and Wanerman, Leon. *Children in Treatment: A Primer for the Beginning Psychotherapist.* New York: Brunner/Mazel, 1977.

Court, Nancy. "The 'Time Line': A Treatment Tool for Children." *Social Work* 25 (May 1980).

Denadello, Gloria. "Some Applications of Ego Psychology Theory to Practice and Programs in Child Welfare." *Child Welfare* 46 (November 1967).

Ebeling, Nancy, and Hill, Deborah, eds. *Child Abuse: Intervention and Treatment.* Acton, Mass.: Publishing Science Group, 1975.

Efron, Donald. "Strategic Therapy Interventions with Latency-Age Children." *Social Casework* 62 (November 1981).

Ewalt, Patricia. "Crisis-Treatment Approach in a Child Guidance Clinic." *Social Casework* 54 (July 1973).

Frank, Margaret. "Casework with Children: The Experience of Treatment." *Smith College Studies in Social Work* 39 (February 1969).

Fuller, Jennie. "Duo-Therapy Case Studies: Process and Treatment." *Social Casework* 58 (February 1977).

Furman, Erna. "Treatment of Under-Fives by Way of Parents." *Psychoanalytic Study of the Child*. New York: International Universities Press, 1957.

Gardner, Richard. *Psychotherapy with Children of Divorce*. New York: Jason Aronson, 1976.

Glickman, Esther. *Child Placement Through Clinically Oriented Casework*. New York: Columbia University Press, 1957.

Goldstein, Joseph; Freud, Anna; and Solnit, Albert. *Before the Best Interests of the Child*. New York: The Free Press, 1980.

_____. *Beyond the Best Interests of the Child*. New York: The Free Press, 1973, and 2d ed., 1980.

Gottlieb, Benjamin, and Gottlieb, Lois. "An Expanded Role for the School Social Worker." *Social Work* 16 (October 1971).

Greenberg, Lois. "Therapeutic Grief Work with Children." *Social Casework* 56 (July 1975).

Grief, Judith. "Fathers, Children, and Joint Custody." *American Journal of Orthopsychiatry* 49 (April 1979).

Holgate, Eileen, ed. *Communicating with Children*. London: Longman, 1972.

Hersch, Alexander. "Changes in Family Functioning." *Social Work* 15 (October 1970).

Jernberg, Ann. *Theraplay: A New Treatment Using Structured Play for Problem Children and Their Families*. San Francisco: Jossey-Bass, 1979.

Johnson, Joy. "School Social Work—A Triangle of Strength." *Journal of School Social Work* 1 (Spring 1974).

Josselyn, Irene. *Psychosocial Development of Children*, 2d ed. New York: Family Service Association of America, 1978.

Kadushin, Alfred. *Child Welfare Services*, 3d ed. New York: Macmillan Co., 1980.

Kempe, C. Henry, and Ray Helfer, eds. *The Battered Child*, 3d ed. Chicago: University of Chicago Press, 1980.

Kempe, Ruth, and Kempe, C. Henry. *Child Abuse*. Cambridge, Mass.: Harvard University Press, 1978.

Kinard, E. Milling. "Mental Health Needs of Abused Children." *Child Welfare* 59 (September-October 1980).

Krieger, Marilyn et al. "Problems in Psychotherapy of Children with Histories of Incest." *American Journal of Psychotherapy* 34 (January 1980).

Krymow, Virginia. "Obstacles Encountered in Permanent Planning for Foster Children." *Child Welfare* 58 (February 1979).

Lieberman, Florence. *Social Work with Children*. New York: Human Sciences Press, 1979.

Littner, Ner. "The Challenge to Make Fuller Use of Our Knowledge about Children." *Child Welfare* 53 (May 1974).

Maluccio, Anthony, and Sinanoglu, Paul. "Social Work With Parents of Children in Foster Care; A Bibliography." *Child Welfare* 60 (May 1981).

Marine, Esther. "School Refusal: Review of the Literature." *Social Service Review* 42 (December 1968).

Pelton, Leroy, ed. *The Social Context of Child Abuse and Neglect*. New York: Human Sciences Press, 1981.

Pike, Victor et al. *Permanent Planning for Children in Foster Care: A Handbook for Social Workers*. Washington, D.C.: Department of Health Education and Welfare, 1977.

Sarnoff, Charles. *Latency*. New York: Jason Aronson, 1976.

Savicki, Victor, and Brown, Rosemary. *Working with Troubled Children*. New York: Human Sciences Press, 1980.

Schaefer, Charles, ed. *Therapeutic Use of Child's Play*. New York: Jason Aronson, 1974.

Schulze, Susanne, ed. *Creative Group Living in a Children's Institution*. New York: Association Press, 1951.

Sherman, Edmund et al. *Service to Children in Their Own Homes: Its Nature and Outcome*. New York: Child Welfare League of America, 1973.

Shyne, Ann, ed. *Child Welfare Perspectives: Selected Papers of Joseph H. Reid*. New York: Child Welfare League of America, 1979.

Silverman, Arnold, and Feigelman, William. "The Adjustment of Black Children Adopted by White Families." *Social Casework* 62 (November 1981).

Stein, Theodore. *Social Work Practice in Child Welfare*. Englewood Cliffs, N.J.: Prentice-Hall, 1981.

71

Stephenson, Susan. "Working with 9- to 12-Year-Old Children." *Child Welfare* 52 (June 1973).

Swanson, Florence. *Psychotherapists and Children: A Procedural Guide.* New York: Pitman Publishing, 1970.

Sundel, Martin, and Homan, Carolyn. "Prevention in Child Welfare: A Framework for Practice and Management." *Child Welfare* 57 (September 1979).

Tooley, Kay. "The Young Child as Victim of Sibling Attack." *Social Casework* 58 (January 1977).

Trieschman, Albert; Whittaker, James; and Brendfro, Larry. *The Other 23 Hours.* Chicago: Aldine Publishing, 1969.

Tsukada, Grace. "Sibling Interaction—A Review of the Literature." *Smith College Studies in Social Work* 49 (June 1979).

Walker, Sydney, III. "Drugging the American Child: We're Too Cavalier About Hyperactivity." *Psychology Today* 8 (December 1974).

Winchell, Carol, comp. *The Hyperkinetic Child: An Annotated Bibliography, 1974–1979.* Westport, Conn.: Greenwood Press, 1981.

Younghusband, Eileen, ed. *Casework with Families and Children.* Chicago: University of Chicago Press, 1966.

B. ADOLESCENTS

Anderson, James, and Brown, Ralph. "Life History Grid for Adolescents." *Social Work* 25 (July 1980).

Bell, Ruth, et al. *Changing Bodies and Changing Lives: A Book for Teens on Sex and Relationships.* New York: Random House, 1980.

Berman, Sidney. "Psychotherapeutic Techniques with Adolescents." *American Journal of Orthopsychiatry* 24 (April 1954).

Blos, Peter. *On Adolescence.* New York: The Free Press, 1962.

——. "The Second Individuation Process of Adolescence." *Psychoanalytic Study of the Child* 22 (1967).

Bolen, Jane. "Easing the Pain of Termination for Adolescents." *Social Casework* 53 (November 1972).

Cain, Lillian. "Social Worker's Role in Teenage Abortions." *Social Work* 24 (January 1979).

Caplan, Gerald, and Lebovich, S., eds. *Psychosocial Perspectives.* New York and London: Basic Books, 1969.

Caroff, Phyllis; Lieberman, Florence; and Gottesfeld, Mary. "The Drug Problem: Treating Preaddictive Adolescents." *Social Casework* 51 (November 1970).

Cartoof, Virginia. "Postpartum Services for Adolescent Mothers." *Child Welfare* 57 (December 1978).

Chilman, Catherine. "Teenage Pregnancy: A Research Review." *Social Work* 24 (November 1979).

Cross, Andra. "The Black Experience: Its Importance in the Treatment of Black Clients." *Child Welfare* 53 (March 1974).

DenHouter, Kathryn. "To Silence One's Self: A Brief Analysis of the Literature on Adolescent Suicide." *Child Welfare* 60 (June 1981).

Dublin, Richard. "Concurrent Group and Family Treatment for Young Adults." *Social Casework* 62 (December 1981).

Enos, Richard, and Hisanaga, Mary. "Goal Setting with Pregnant Teenagers." *Child Welfare* 58 (September/October 1979).

Gilbert, Gwendolyn. "Counseling Black Adolescent Parents." *Social Work* 19 (January 1974).

Ginott, Haim. *Between Parent and Teenager*. New York: Avon Books. 1969.

Group for the Advancement of Psychiatry. Report no. 68. *Normal Adolescence*. New York: Charles Scribner, 1968.

Hartmann, Ernest et al. *Adolescents in a Mental Hospital*. New York: Grune and Stratton, 1968.

Highland, Anne. "Depression in Adolescents: A Developmental View." *Child Welfare* 58 (November 1979).

Homer, Louise. "Community Based Resource for Runaway Girls." *Social Casework* 54 (October 1973).

Johnson, Adelaide. "Sanctions for Superego Lacunae of Adolescence." In *Searchlights on Delinquency*. Edited by K. R. Eissler. New York: International Universities Press, 1949.

Johnson, Carolyn; Walters, Lynda; and McKenry, Patrick. "Trends in Services for Pregnant Adolescents." *Health and Social Work* 43 (August 1979).

Jones, Ray, and Cohen, Pritchard, eds. *Social Work with Adolescents*. Boston, Mass.: Routledge and Kegan Paul, 1981.

Josselyn, Irene. "Value Problems in the Treatment of Adolescents." *Smith College Studies in Social Work* 42 (November 1971).

Kerns, Elizabeth. "Planned Short-Term Treatment, a New Service to Adolescents." *Social Casework* 51 (June 1970). Also in *Differential Diagnosis and Treatment in Social Work*. Edited by Francis Turner. New York: The Free Press, 1968, 2d ed. 1976.

Konopka, Gisela. *The Adolescent Girl in Conflict*. Englewood Cliffs, N.J.: Prentice-Hall, 1966.

Kovar, Lillian. *Faces of the Adolescent Girl*. Englewood Cliffs, N.J.: Prentice-Hall, 1966.

La Barre, Weston. "Adolescence, the Crucible of Change." *Social Casework* 50 (January 1969).

Laufer, Moses. "Ego Ideal and Pseudo Ego Ideal in Adolescence." *Psychoanalytic Study of the Child* 21 (1964).

————. "Object Loss and Mourning During Adolescence." *Psychoanalytic Study of the Child* 21 (1964).

Levinson, Hilliard. "Communication with an Adolescent in Psychotherapy." *Social Casework* 54 (October 1973).

McLaney, Martha. "Casework with a Troubled Teen-ager and Drug Abuser." *Social Casework* 52 (November 1971).

Maier, Henry. "Adolescenthood." *Social Casework* 46 (January 1965).

Maultsby, Maxie, Jr. "Rational Behavior Therapy for Acting-Out Adolescents." *Social Casework* 56 (January 1975).

Meeks, John. *The Fragile Alliance: An Orientation to the Out-Patient Psychotherapy of the Adolescent*. Baltimore: Williams and Wilkins, 1971.

Meyers, H. "The Therapist's Response to Today's Adolescent." *Psychosocial Process* 2 (1971).

Nichols, William Jr., and Rutledge, Aaron. "Psychotherapy with Teenagers." *Journal of Marriage and the Family* 27 (May 1965).

Norman, Jennie. "Short-Term Treatment with the Adolescent Client." *Social Casework* 61 (February 1980).

Phillips, Gary. "The Centrality of Autonomy in Psychotherapy with the Adolescent." *Child Welfare* 49 (February 1970).

Rabichow, Helen. "Casework Treatment of Adolescents with Learning Inhibitions." *Social Work* 8 (October 1963). Also in Turner's *Differential Diganosis and Treatment*.

Scherz, Frances. "The Crisis of Adolescence in Family Life." *Social Casework* 48 (April 1967).

Schlachter, Roy. "Home Counseling of Adolescents and Parents." *Social Work* 20 (November 1975).

Settlage, Calvin. "Cultural Values and the Superego in Late Adolescence." *Psychoanalytic Study of the Child* (1972).

Sprince, Marjorie, and Baker, S. "Work with Adolescents: Brief Psychotherapy with a Limited Aim." *Journal of Child Psychotherapy* 2 (1968).

Sugar, Max. "Normal Adolescent Mourning." *American Journal of Psychotherapy* 22 (April 1968).

Turner, Francis, ed. *Differential Diagnosis and Treatment in Social Work.* New York: The Free Press, 1968. (Five articles on treatment of adolescents.) 2d ed., 1976. (Three additional articles on treatment of adolescents.)

C. YOUNG ADULTS

Alexander, Janette. "Alternative Life Styles: Relationship Between New Realities and Practice." *Clinical Social Work Journal* 4 (Winter 1976).

Amada, Gerald, and Swartz, Jacqueline. "Social Work in a College Mental Health Program." *Social Casework* 53 (November 1972).

Barnett, Joseph. "Dependency Conflicts in the Young Adult." *Psychoanalytic Review* 58 (Spring 1971).

Barnhill, Laurence, and Long, Dianne. "Fixation and Regression in the Family Life Cycle." *Family Process* 17 (December 1978).

Benney, Celia et al. "Facilitating Functioning of Mentally Ill Young Adults." *Social Casework* 52 (July 1971).

Dublin, Richard. "Concurrent Group and Family Treatment for Young Adults." *Social Casework* 62 (December 1981).

Erikson, Erik. *Adulthood.* New York: W.W. Norton and Co., 1978.
———. *Childhood and Society.* See especially Chap. 7, "Eight Stages of Man." New York: W.W. Norton, 1950.

Gibbs, Jewella. "Use of Mental Health Services by Black Students at a Predominantly White University: A Three Year Study." *American Journal of Orthopsychiatry* 45 (April 1975).

Glenn, Clifford, and Odin, Katherine. "Young Adulthood: A Developmental Phase." *Smith College Studies in Social Work* 44 (February 1974).

Gould, Roger. "The Phases in Adult Life: A Study in Developmental Psychology." *American Journal of Psychiatry* 129 (November 1972).

Harris, Gloria, and Wagner, Nathaniel. "Treatment of Sexual
Dysfunction and Casework Techniques." *Clinical Social Work
Journal* 1 (Winter 1973). Special Issue on Modern Sexuality.
Hartman, Susan, and Hynes, Jane. "Marriage Education for Mentally
Retarded Adults." *Social Casework* 56 (May 1975).
Irving, Howard. "Relationships Between Married Couples and Their
Parents." *Social Casework* 52 (February 1971).
Isaacson, June, and Delgado, Harriet. "Sex Counseling for Those
with Spinal Cord Injuries." *Social Casework* 55 (December 1974).
Jolesch, Miriam. "Casework Treatment of Young Married Couples."
In *Differential Diagnosis and Treatment in Social Work*. Edited by
Francis Turner. New York: The Free Press, 1968, 2d ed. 1976.
Kaplan, Mildred. "Counseling Middle-Class University Students."
Social Casework 55 (October 1974).
Leader, Arthur. "Denied Dependency in Family Therapy." *Social
Casework* 57 (December 1976).
_____. "The Place of In-laws in Marital Relationships." *Social
Casework* 56 (October 1975).
Levinson, Daniel. "Growing Up with the Dream." *Psychology Today*
11 (January 1978).
Lidz, Theodore. *The Person*. New York: Basic Books. 1976. See
especially Chap. 11, "The Young Adult"; Chap. 12; "Occupational
Choice"; Chap. 13, "Marital Choice"; Chap. 14, "Marital
Adjustment"; and Chap. 15, "Parenthood."
Nadelson, Carol et al. "Evaluation Procedures for Conjoint Marital
Psychotherapy." *Social Casework* 56 (February 1975).
Perlman, Helen. *Persona, Social Role and Responsibility*. Chicago:
University of Chicago Press, 1968.
Pincus, Cynthia et al. "A Professional Counseling Service for
Women." *Social Work* 19 (March 1974).
Rosenberg, Blanca. "Planned Short-Term Treatment in
Developmental Crises." *Social Casework* 56 (April 1975).
Rustin, Judith, and Nathanson, Robert. "Integrating Disabled
Students into a College Population." *Social Casework* 56
(November 1975).
Schild, Sylvia. "Social Workers' Contribution to Genetic
Counseling." *Social Casework* 54 (July 1973).
Sheehy, Gail. *Passages: Predictable Crises of Adult Life*. New York:
E.P. Dutton, 1974.
Silver, Steven. "Outpatient Treatment for Sexual Offenders." *Social
Work* 21 (March 1976).

Vaillant, George. "The Climb and Maturity: How the Best and
Brightest Came to Age." *Psychology Today* 11 (September 1977).

D. THE MIDDLE YEARS

Borgman, Robert. "Medication Abuse by Middle-Aged Women."
Social Casework 54 (November 1973).
Cath, Stanley. "Some Dynamics of Middle and Later Years: A Study
in Depletion and Restitution." *Smith College Studies in Social
Work* 35 (February 1965). Also in *Crises Intervention: Selected
Readings*. Edited by Howard Parad. New York: Family Service
Association of America, 1965.
Deykin, Eva et al. "The Empty Nest: Psychosocial Aspects of
Conflicts Between Depressed Women and Their Grown
Children." *American Journal of Psychiatry* 122 (June 1966).
Klass, Shirley, and Redfern, Margaret. "A Social Work Response to
the Middle-Aged Housewife." *Social Casework* 58 (February
1977).
Martin, Robert, and Prosen, Harry. "Psychotherapy Supervision and
Life Tasks: The Young Therapist and the Middle-Aged Patient."
Bulletin of the Menninger Clinic 40 (March 1976).
Miller, Dorothy. "The Sandwich Generation: Adult Children of the
Aging." *Social Work* 26 (September 1981).
Neugarten, Bernice, ed. *Middle Age and Aging*. Chicago: University
of Chicago Press, 1968.
Wasserman, Sidney. "The Middle-Age Separation Crisis and Ego
Supportive Casework Treatment." *Clinical Social Work Journal*
(Spring 1973). Also in Turner's *Differential Diagnosis and
Treatment in Social Work*. Edited by Francis Turner. New York:
The Free Press, 1968, and 2d ed., 1976.
Zachs, Hanna. "Self-Actualization: A Midlife Problem." *Social
Casework* 61 (April 1980).

E. THE AGED

Beaulieu, Elsie, and Karpinski, Judith. "Group Treatment of Elderly
with Ill Spouses." *Social Casework* 62 (November 1981).
Berger, Raymond, and Piliavin, Irving. "The Effect of Casework on
the Aged." *Social Work* 21 (May 1976).

Berkman, Barbara. "Mental Health and the Aging: A Review of the
Literature for Clinical Social Workers." *Clinical Social Work
Journal* 6 (Fall 1976).
Birren, James, ed. *Relation of Development and Aging.* Springfield,
Ill.: Charles C Thomas Publishing Co., 1964. See especially "A
Developmental View of Adult Personality."
Bradford, Leland, and Bradford, Martha. *Retirement: Coping With
Emotional Upheavals.* Chicago: Nelson-Hall, 1981.
Butler, R., and Lewis, M. *Aging and Mental Health: Positive
Psychosocial Approaches.* St. Louis, Mo.: C. V. Mosby Co., 1973.
Cath, Stanley. "Some Dynamics of Middle and Later Years: A Study
in Depletion and Restitution." *Smith College Studies in Social
Work* 35 (February 1965). Also in *Crisis Intervention: Selected
Readings.* Edited by Howard Parad. New York: Family Service
Association of America, 1965.
Cohen, Ruth. "Outreach and Advocay in the Treatment of the Aged."
Social Casework 55 (May 1974).
Cook, Alicia. "A Model for Working with the Elderly in Institutions."
Social Casework 62 (September 1981).
Cormican, Elin. "A Task-Centered Model for Work with the Aged."
Social Casework 58 (October 1977).
English, O. Spurgeon, and Pearson, Gerald. *Emotional Problems of
Living Avoiding the Neurotic Pattern.* New York: W.W. Norton,
1955. See especially "Maturity and Its Problems."
Ford, Caroline. "Ego-Adaptive Mechanisms of Older Persons."
Social Casework 46 (January 1965).
Golan, Naomi. "Wife to Widow to Woman." *Social Work* 20 (May
1975).
Kalish, Richard. *Late Adulthood: Perspectives on Human
Development.* Berkeley, Calif.: Brooks/Cole, 1975.
Kastenbaum, Robert. "The Reluctant Therapist." *Geriatrics* 18 (April
1963).
Kent, Donald et al., eds. *Research, Planning and Action for the
Elderly.* New York: Behavioral Publications, 1972.
Kulys, Regina and Tobin, Sheldon. "Older People and Their
'Responsible Others' ". *Social Work* 25 (March 1980).
Leach, Jean. "Intergenerational Approach in Casework with the
Aging." *Social Casework* 45 (March 1964).
Levin, Sydney. "Depression in the Aged." In *Geriatric Psychiatry.*
Edited by Martin A. Berezin and Stanley Cath. New York:
International Universities Press, 1967.

Milloy, Margaret. "Casework with the Older Person and His Family." *Social Casework* 45 (October 1964). Also in *Differential Diagnosis and Treatment in Social Work*. Edited by Francis Turner. New York: The Free Press, 1968, and 2d ed., 1976.

Monk, Abraham. *The Age of Aging: A Reader in Social Gerontolgy*. Buffalo, N.Y.: Prometheus Books, 1979.

————. "Social Work With the Aged: Principles and Practice." *Social Work* 26 (January 1981).

Neugarten, Bernice, ed. *Middle Age and Aging*. Chicago: University of Chicago Press, 1968.

Pincus, Allen. "Reminiscence in Aging and Its Implications for Social Work Practice." *Social Work* 15 (July 1970).

————. "Toward a Developmental View of Aging for Social Work." *Social Work* 12 (July 1967).

Sander, Faye. "Aspects of Sexual Counseling with the Aged." *Social Casework* 57 (October 1976).

Sheldon, A. et al. *Retirement: Patterns and Predictions*. Washington, D.C.: National Institute of Mental Health, 1975. See Section on "Mental Health of the Aging."

Shura, Saul. *Aging: An Album of People Growing Old*. New York: John Wiley and Sons, 1974.

Skelskie, Barbara. "Grief in Old Age." *Smith College Studies in Social Work* 45 (February 1975).

Soyer David. "Reverie on Working with the Aged." *Social Casework* 50 (May 1969). Also in Turner's *Differential Diagnosis and Treatment* (See entry under Milloy above.)

Spark, Geraldine. "Grandparents and Intergenerational Family Therapy." *Family Process* 13 (June 1974).

Wetzel, Janice. "Interventions With the Depressed Elderly in Institutions." *Social Casework* 61 (April 1980).

F. WOMEN

Bart, Pauline. "Depression in Middle-Aged Women." In *Woman in Sexist Society*. Edited by Vivian Gornick and Barbara K. Moran. New York: Basic Books, 1971.

Bass, David, and Rice, Janet. "Agency Responses to the Abused Wife." *Social Casework* 60 (June 1979).

Becket, Joyce. "Working Wives: A Racial Comparison." *Social Work* 21 (November 1976).

Berlin, Sharon. "Better Work with Women Clients." *Social Work* 21 (November 1976).

Bernard, Jessie. *Women, Wives, Mothers.* Chicago: Aldine Publishing, 1975.

The Black Scholar 3 (December 1971). Entire issue focused on the black woman.

Borg, Susan and Lasker, Judith. *When Pregnancy Fails: Families Coping with Miscarriage, Stillbirth and Infant Death."* Boston, Mass.: Beacon Press, 1981.

Broverman, Inge et al. "Sex-Role Stereotypes and Clinical Judgments of Mental Health." *Journal of Consulting and Clinical Psychology* 34 (February 1970).

Brown, Caree, and Hellinger, Marilyn. "Therapists' Attitudes Toward Women." *Social Work* 20 (July 1975).

The Boston Women's Health Book Collective. *Our Bodies, Ourselves.* 2d ed. New York: Simon and Schuster, 1976.

Buttrick, Shirley, and Rivera-Martinez, Carmen, eds. *Feminism and Families: Real or Presumed Conflicts.* Chicago: Jane Addams School of Social Work, 1978.

Carlson, Rae. "Understanding Women: Implications for Personality Theory and Research." *Journal of Social Issues* 28 (1972).

Chafetz, Janet. "Women in Social Work." *Social Work* 17 (September 1972).

Chapman, Jane, and Gates, Margaret. *The Victimization of Women.* Beverly Hills, Calif.: Sage Publications, 1978.

Chester, Phyllis. "Patient and Patriarch: Women in the Psychotherapeutic Relationship." In Gornick and Moran's *Women in Sexist Society*1 (See entry under Bart above.)

Daedalus. 3 (Spring 1964). Entire issue focused on women.

Davenport, Judith, and Reims, Nancy. "Theoretical Orientation and Attitudes Towards Women." *Social Work* 23 (July 1978).

Dobash, R. Emerson, and Dobash, Russell. *Violence Against Wives: A Case Against the Patriarchy.* New York: The Free Press, 1979

Epstein, Cynthia. "Women's Attitudes Toward Other Women—Myths and Their Consequences." *American Journal of Psychotherapy* 34 (July 1980).

Gottlieb, Naomai, ed. *New Knowledge About Women: A Selected Annotated Bibliography for the Human Behavior and Social Environment Curriculum on Social Work Education.* New York: Council on Social Work Education, 1981.

Higgins, John. "Social Services for Abused Wives." *Social Casework* 59 (May 1978).

Joffe, Carole. "Abortion Work: Strains, Coping Strategies, Policy Implications." *Social Work* 24 (November 1979).

Lerner, Gerda. *Black Women in White America.* New York: Pantheon, 1972.

Marmor, Judd. "Changing Patterns of Femininity." In *Family in Transition.* Edited by Jerome and Arlene Skolnick. Boston: Little, Brown and Co., 1971.

Martin, Del. *Battered Wives.* San Francisco: Glide Publications. See also *Ms.* 5 (August 1976).

Miller, Donna. "The Influence of the Patient's Sex on Clinical Judgment." *Smith College Studies in Social Work* 44 (March 1974).

Miller, Jean. *Psychoanalysis and Women.* New York: Brunner/Mazel, 1973.

Mostow, Evelyn, and Newberry, P. "Work Role and Depression in Women: A Comparison of Workers and Housewives in Treatment." *American Journal of Orthopsychiatry* 45 (July 1975).

Nichols, Beverly. "The Abused Wife Problem." *Social Casework* 57 (January 1976).

_____. "Motherhood, Mothering, and Casework." *Social Casework* 58 (January 1977).

Norman, Elaine, and Mancuso, Arlene. *Women's Issues and Social Work Practice.* Itasca, Ill.: F.E. Peacock, 1980.

Schwartz, Mary. "Importance of the Sex of Worker and Client." *Social Work* 19 (March 1974).

Shainess, Natalie. "The Working Wife and Mother—A 'New' Woman?" *American Journal of Psychotherapy* 34 (July 1980).

Social Work 21 (November 1976). Entire issue focused on women.

Steinmetz, Suzanne. "Women and Violence: Victims and Perpetrators." *American Journal of Psychotherapy* 34 (July 1980).

Walker, Lenore. *The Battered Woman.* New York: Harper and Row, 1979.

Wattenberg, Esther, and Reinhardt, Hazel. "Female Headed Families: Trends and Implications." *Social Work* 24 (November 1979).

Weick, Ann et al. *An Alternative Resource Bibliography on Women.* New York: Council on Social Work Education, 1981.

Wesley, Carol. "The Women's Movement and Psychotherapy." *Social Work* 20 (March 1975).

Wortis, Helen, and Rubinowitz, Clara, eds. *The Women's Movement: Social and Psychological Perspectives.* New York: AMS Press, 1974.

Zimmerman, Mary. *Passage Through Abortion: The Personal and Social Reality of Women's Experiences.* New York: Praeger Publishers, 1977.

Zukerman, Elyse. *Changing Directions in the Treatment of Women: A Mental Health Bibliography.* Rockville, Md.: Department of Health, Education and Welfare, National Institute of Mental Health, 1979.

G. MINORITIES

See also sections under Exploration and Assessment: Social and Economic Factors, and Racial, Ethnic, and Cultural Factors. Many of these articles relate to intervention as well as assessment.

Aguilar, Ignacio. "Initial Contacts with Mexican-American Families." *Social Work* 17:3 (May 1972). Also in *Differential Diagnosis and Treatment in Social Work.* Edited by Francis Turner. New York: The Free Press, 1968, 2d ed., 1976.

Brown, John. "Clinical Social Work with Chicanos: Some Unwarranted Assumptions." *Clinical Social Work Journal* 7 (Winter 1979).

Cadie, Brian. "Therapy with Low Socio-Economic Families." *Social Work Today* 6 (May 1975).

Chethik, Morton et al. "A Quest for Identity: Treatment of Disturbed Negro Children." *American Journal of Orthopsychiatry* 27 (January 1967).

Delgado, Melvin. "Accepting Folk Healers: Problems and Rewards." *Journal of Social Welfare* 6 (Fall-Winter 1979–80).

_____. "Using Hispanic Adolescents to Assess Community Needs." *Social Casework* 62 (December 1981).

Gochros, Jean. "Recognition and Use of Anger in Negro Clients." *Social Work* 11 (January 1966).

Hallowitz, David. "Counseling and Treatment of the Poor Black Family." *Social Casework* 56 (October 1975).

Hardy-Fanta, Carol, and MacMahon-Herrera, Elizabeth. "Adapting Family Therapy to the Hispanic Family." *Social Casework* 62 (March 1981).

Henderson, George, ed. *Understanding and Counseling Ethnic Minorities*. Springfield, Ill.: Charles C Thomas, 1979.

Hopkins, Thomas. "The Role of the Agency in Supporting Black Manhood." *Social Work* 18 (January 1973).

Hostbjor, Stella. "Social Services to the Indian (American) Unwed Mother." *Child Welfare* 40 (May 1961).

Jones, Darielle. "African-American Clients: Clinical Practice Issues." *Social Work* 24 (March 1979).

LaBarre, Maurine, and LaBarre, Weston. "The Worm in the Honeysuckle: A Case of a Child's Hysterical Blindness." *Social Casework* 46 (July 1965).

Mayo, J. "The Significance of Socio-Cultural Variables in the Psychiatric Treatment of Black Out-patients." *Comprehensive Psychiatry* 15 (November-December 1974).

Medina, Celia, and Reyes, Maria. "Dilemmas of Chicana Counselors." *Social Work* 21 (November 1976).

Mizio, Emelicia, and Delaney, Anita. eds. *Training for Service Delivery to Minority Clients*. New York: Family Service Association of America, 1981.

Oliver, John, and Lukens, Janet. "Ethnocentrism and Communicative Distances: Barriers to Effective Interracial Interaction Within Clinical Settings." *Journal of Social Welfare* 6 (Summer-Fall 1979).

Pederson, Paul et al., eds. *Counseling Across Cultures, Revised and Expanded Edition*. Honolulu: University Press of Hawaii, 1981.

Sager, Clifford et al. *Black Ghetto Family in Therapy*. New York: Grove Press, 1970.

Silverman, Arnold, and Feigelman, William. "The Adjustment of Black Children Adopted by White Families." *Social Casework* 62 (November 1981).

Social Casework. Entire issue on blacks and racism. 52 (May 1970).

Sue, Derald, and Sue, David. "Barriers to Effective Cross-Cultural Counseling." *Journal of Counseling Psychology* 24 (September 1977).

Tyler, Inez, and Thompson, Sophie. "Cultural Factors in Casework Treatment of a Navajo Mental Patient." *Social Casework* 46 (April 1965). Also in Turner's *Differential Diagnosis and Treatment*. (See entry under Aguilar above.)

Williams, Constance. "Issues in the Treatment of Black Families." *Smith College Studies in Social Work* 50 (June 1980).

H. PHYSICAL HEALTH AND ILLNESS

1. GENERAL CONSIDERATIONS

Abram, Harry. "The Psychology of Chronic Illness." *Journal of Chronic Diseases* 25 (March 1972).

Adams, John, and Lindemann, Erich. "Coping with Long Term Disability." In *Coping and Adaptation*. Edited by G. V. Coelho et al. New York: Basic Books, 1974.

Alexander, Franz. *Psychosomatic Medicine: Its Principles and Applications*. New York: W.W. Norton, 1950.

Anthony, E. James. "Mutative Impact of Serious Mental and Physical Illness in a Parent on Family Life." In *The Child in His Family*. Edited by E. James Anthony and Cyrille Koupernik, New York: John Wiley and Sons, 1970.

Babcock, Charlotte. "Inner Stress in Illness and Disability." In *Ego-Oriented Casework: Problems and Perspectives—Papers from the Smith College School for Social Work*. Edited by Howard Parad and Roger Miller. New York: Family Service Association of America, 1973.

Bartlett, Harriett. *The Common Base of Social Work Practice*. New York: National Association of Social Workers, 1970.

_____. *Social Work Practice in the Health Field*. New York: National Association of Social Workers, 1961.

Bender, Barbara. "Management of Acute Hospitalization Anxiety." *Social Casework* 57 (January 1976).

Bergman, Anne Sturmthal. "Emergency Room: A Role for Social Worker." *Health and Social Work* 1 (February 1976).

Berkman, Barbara, and Rehr, Helen. "The 'Sick-role' Cycle and the Timing of Social Work Intervention." *Social Service Review* 46 (December 1972).

Bernstein, Barton. "Legal Needs of the Ill: The Social Worker's Role on an Interdisciplinary Team." *Health and Social Work* 5 (August 1980).

Bracht, Neil. "Health Care: The Largest Human Service System." *Social Work* 19 (September 1974).

_____. *Social Work in Health Care: A Guide to Professional Practice*. New York: Haworth Press, 1978.

Cameron, Norman. *Personality Development and Psychopathology: A Dynamic Approach*. Boston: Houghton Mifflin, 1963. See especially Chap. 20, "Psychosomatic Disorders."

Chernesky, Roslyn, and Lurie, Abraham. "Developing a Quality Assurance Program." *Health and Social Work* 1 (February 1976).

Coulton, Claudia. "A Study of Person-Environment Fit Among the Chronically Ill." *Social Work in Health Care*. 5 (Fall 1979).

Cowin, Ruth et al. "Social Work in a Child Health Clinic: A Report of a Demonstration." *American Journal of Public Health* 55 (June 1965).

"Doing Better and Feeling Worse: Health in the U.S." *Daedalus*. 106 (Winter, 1977).

Fuchs, Victor. *Who Shall Live?* New York: Basic Books, 1975.

Gentry, Veney et al. "The Adoption of Social Work Services by Hospitals and Health Departments." *American Journal of Public Health* 63 (February 1973).

Goldberg, Stanley. "Family Tasks and Reactions in the Crisis of Death." *Social Casework* 54 (July 1973).

Goldstein, Eda. "Social Casework and the Dying Person." *Social Casework* 54 (December 1973).

Hutter, Maureen; Zakus, Gloria; and Dungy, Clairborne. "Social Work Training of New Health Professionals." *Health and Social Work* 1 (May 1976).

Jackson, Robert, and Morton, Jean, eds. *Family Health Care: Health Promotion and Illness Care*. Berkeley: University of California, School of Public Health, 1976.

Jaco, E. Gartly, ed. *Patients, Physicians and Illness*. New York: The Free Press, 1972.

Kaplan, David et al. "Family Mediation of Stress." *Social Work* 18 (July 1973).

Krell, George. "Overstay Among Hospital Patients, Problems and Approaches." *Health and Social Work* 2 (February 1977).

Krupp, George. "Maladaptive Reactions to the Death of a Family Member." *Social Casework* 53 (July 1972).

Kübler-Ross, Elisabeth. *On Death and Dying*. New York: Macmillan Co., 1971.

Lidz, Theodore. "General Concepts of Psychosomatic Medicine." In *American Handbook of Psychiatry*. Edited by Silvano Arieti. New York: Basic Books, 1959.

Lucente, Frank, and Fleck, Stephen. "A Study of Hospitalization Anxiety in 408 Medical and Surgical Patients." *Psychosomatic Medicine* 34 (July-August 1972).

Lum, Doman. "The Social Service Health Specialist in a Health Maintenance Organization." *Health and Social Work* 1 (May 1976).

Mailick, Mildred. "The Impact of Severe Illness on the Individual and the Family: An Overview." *Social Work in Health Care* 5 (Winter 1979).

Morris, Robert, and Anderson, Delvin. "Personal Care Services: An Identity for Social Work." *Social Service Review* 49 (June 1975).

Nichiura, Eleanor; Witten, Charles; and Jenkins, Dorothy. "Screening for Psychosocial Problems in Health Settings." *Health and Social Work* 5 (August 1980).

Norton, Janice. "Treatment of the Dying Patient." *Psychoanalytic Study of the Child* 18 (1963).

Parkins, Robert; Parker, Jack; and Daste, Barry. "Multiple-Influence Paradigms in Illness." *Social Casework* 56 (November 1975).

Peel, John, and Potts, Malcolm. A *Handbook of Contraceptive Technology*. Cambridge: Cambridge University Press, 1969.

Phillips, Beatrice. "Social Service Programs Require Imaginative Staff Deployment." *Hospitals, Journal of the American Hospital Association* 43 (September 1969).

Reinhez, Berkman, and Ewalt, G. "Training in Accountability: A Social Work Mandate." *Health and Social Work* 2 (May 1977).

Rosenberg, Mark. *Patients: The Experience of Illness*. Philadelphia: Saunders Press, 1980.

Shellhase, Leslie, and Shellhase, Fern. "Role of the Family in Rehabilitation." *Social Casework* 53 (November 1972).

Social Work Activities in Public Health: Report of a Workshop. Boston: Massachusetts Department of Public Health, 1961.

Spiegel, John. "Cultural Variations in Attitudes Toward Death and Disease." In *The Threat of Impending Disaster*. Edited by George Grosser, Henry Wechsler, and Milton Greenblatt. Cambridge, Mass.: Massachusetts Institute of Technology, 1964.

Stein, Edward; Mordaugh, Jessie; and MacLeod, John. "Brief Psychotherapy of Psychiatric Reactions to Physical Illness." In *Brief Therapies*. Edited by Harvey Barton. New York: Behavioral Publications, 1971.

Thale, Thomas. "Effects of Medication on the Caseworker-Client Relationship." *Social Casework* 54 (January 1973).

Vernick, Joel. "The Use of the Life-Space Interview on a Medical Ward." In *Crisis Intervention: Selected Readings*. Edited by Howard Parad. New York: Family Service Association of America, 1965.

Weisberg, Lillian. "Casework with the Terminally Ill." *Social Casework* 55 (June 1974).

Whittington, Ronaele. "Social Services for a Nursing Home: A Collaboration Approach." *Health and Social Work* 2 (May 1977).

Zborowski, Mark. "Cultural Components in Response to Pain." *Journal of Social Issues* 8 (1952). Also in Jaco's *Patients, Physicians, and Illness*.

_____. *People in Pain*. San Francisco: Jossey-Bass, 1969.

2. SPECIFIC ILLNESSES IN ADULTS

Abrams, Ruth. *Not Alone with Cancer*. Springfield, Ill.: Charles C Thomas, 1974.

_____. "Social Casework with Cancer Patients." *Social Casework* 32 (December 1951).

Atcherson, Ester. "The Quality of Life: A Study of Hemodialysis Patients." *Health and Social Work* 3 (November 1978).

Bondy, Magda. "Casework with Families and Patients Facing Cardiovascular Surgery." In *Differential Diagnosis and Treatment in Social Work*. Edited by Francis Turner. New York: The Free Pres, 1968, 2d ed., 1976.

Bruch, Hilde. *Eating Disorders: Obesity, Anorexia Nervosa and the Person Within*. New York: Basic Books, 1973.

Chrzanowski, Gerard. "Neurasthenia and Hypochondriasis." In *American Handbook of Psychiatry*. Edited by Silvano Arieti. New York: Basic Books, 1959.

Domanski, Margaret, et al. "Comprehensive Care of the Chronically Ill Cancer Patient: An Inter-Agency Model." *Social Work in Health Care* 5 (Fall 1979).

Engelmann, Mary. "The Diabetic Client." In Turner's *Differential Diagnosis and Treatment*. (See entry under Bondy above.)

Ezra, Julia. "Casework in a Coronary Care Unit." *Social Casework* 50 (May 1969).

Hickey, Kathleen. "Impact on Kidney Disease on Patient, Family and Society." *Social Casework* 53 (July 1972).

Jablon, Rosalind, and Vol, Herbert. "Revealing Diagnosis and Prognosis to Cancer Patients." In Turner's *Differential Diagnosis and Treatment*. (See entry under Bondy above.)

Knapp, Peter. "The Asthmatic and His Environment." *Journal of Nervous and Mental Disease* 149 (August 1969).

Linden, George. "The Influence of Social Class in the Survival of Cancer Patients." *American Journal of Public Health* 59 (February 1969).

MacKinnon, Robert, and Michels, Robert. *The Psychiatric Interview in Clinical Practice*. Philadelphia: W. B. Saunders Co., 1971. See especially Chap. 11, "The Psychosomatic Patient."

MacNamara, Margaret. "The Family in Stress: Social Work Before and After Renal Hemotransplantation." *Social Work* 14 (October 1969).

Nelsen, Judith. "Treatment of Patients with Minor Psychosomatic Disorders." *Social Casework* 50 (December 1969).

Obier, Kathleen, and Haywood, L. Julian. "Role of the Medical Social Worker in a Coronary Care Unit." *Social Casework* 53 (January 1972).

Oppenheimer, Jeannette. "Use of Crisis Intervention in Casework with the Cancer Patient." *Social Work* 12 (April 1967).

Schoenberg, Bernard, and Carr, Arthur. "Loss of External Organs: Limb Amputations, Mastectomy and Disfiguration." In *Loss and Grief: Psychological Management in Medical Practice*. Edited by Bernard Schoenberg et al. New York: Columbia University Press, 1970.

Senescu, Robert. "The Development of Emotional Complications in the Patient with Cancer." *Journal of Chronic Diseases* 16 (July 1963).

Sheldon, Alan; Ryser, Carol; and Krant, Melvin. "An Integrated Family Oriented Cancer Care Program: The Report of a Pilot Project in the Socio-Emotional Management of Chronic Disease." *Journal of Chronic Diseases* 22 (April 1970).

Smith, Larry. "Helping to Manage the Emotional Effects of Arthritis." *Health and Social Work* 4 (August 1979).

3. ILLNESSES IN CHILDREN

Blom, Gaston. "The Reaction of Hospitalized Children to Illness." *Pediatrics* 22 (September 1958).

Bruch, Hilde. *The Golden Cage: The Enigma of Anorexia Nervosa.* Cambridge, Mass.: Harvard University Press, 1978.

Brueton, Mary. "Casework with Asthmatic Children." In *Differential Diagnosis and Treatment in Social Work.* Edited by Francis Turner. New York: The Free Press, 1968, 2d ed., 1976.

Casework Services for Parents of Handicapped Children. Reprints from *Social Casework.* New York: Family Service Association of America, 1963.

Chodoff, Paul; Friedman, Stanford; and Hamburg, David. "Stress, Defense and Copying Behavior Observations in Parents of Children with Malignant Disease." *American Journal of Psychiatry* 120 (February 1964).

Gochros, Harvey, and Schultz, LeRoy, eds. *Human Sexuality and Social Work.* New York: Association Press, 1972. See Chap. 14.

Cowin, Ruth. "The Role of the Social Worker: Problems of Impending Death." *Journal of the American Physical Therapy Association* 48 (July 1968).

Freud, Anna. "The Role of Bodily Illness in the Mental Life of Children." *Psychoanalytic Study of the Child* 7 (1952).

Gardner, Richard. "The Guilt Reaction of Parents of Children with Severe Physical Disease." *American Journal of Psychiatry* 126 (November 1969).

Hall, Juanita, and Taylor, Kathleen. "The Emergence of Eric: Co-Therapy in the Treatment of a Family with a Disabled Child." *Family Process* 10 (March 1971).

Hamovitch, M. B. *The Parent and the Fatally Ill Child.* Los Angeles: Delmar Publishers, 1964.

Hill, Emma, and Hynes, Jane. "Fostering Self-Esteem in Families with Diabetic Children." *Child Welfare* 59 (November 1980).

Lang, Priscilla, and Oppenheimer, Jeanette. "The Influence of Social Work When Parents are Faced with the Fatal Illness of a Child." *Social Casework* 49 (March 1968).

Lloyd, Katherine. "Helping a Child Adapt to Stress: The Use of Ego Psychology in Casework." In *Casework with Families and Children*. Edited by Eileen Younghusband. Chicago: Chicago University Press, 1965.

Minuchin, Salvador. "Ecology and Child Therapy." In *The Child in His Family*. Edited by Anthony James, and Cyrille Koupernik. New York: John Wiley and Sons, 1970.

————— et al. "A Conceptual Model of Psychosomatic Illness in Children." *Archives of General Psychiatry* 32 (August 1975).

Morrissey, James. "Death Anxiety in Children with a Fatal Disease." *American Journal of Psychotherapy* 18 (Winter 1964). Also in *Crisis Intervention: Selected Readings*. Edited by Howard Parad. New York: Family Service Association of America, 1965.

Morse, Joan. "Family Involvement in Pediatric Dialysis and Transplantation." *Social Casework* 55 (April 1974).

—————. "Making Hospitalization a Growth Experience for Arthritic Children." In Turner's *Differential Diagnosis and Treatment*. (See entry under Brueton above.)

Reinhart, John; Kenna, Marita; and Succop, Ruth. "Anorexia Nervosa in Children: Out-Patient Arrangement." *Journal of the American Academy of Child Psychiatry* 11 (January 1972).

Ross, Judith. "Social Work Intervention With Families of Children With Cancer: The Changing Critical Phases." *Social Work in Health Care* 3 (Spring 1978).

Sharkey, Clayton, and Taylor, John. "Management of Maladaptive Behavior of a Severely Burned Child." *Child Welfare* 52 (October 1973).

Schultz, Susan. "Compliance With Therapeutic Regimens in Pediatrics." *Social Work in Health Care* 5 (Spring 1980).

Sheridan, Mary. "Psychosomatic Illness in Children." *Social Casework* 59 (April 1978).

I. RETARDATION

Adams, Margaret. *Mental Retardation and Its Social Dimensions*. New York: Columbia University Press, 1971.

Adamson, William et al. "Separation Used to Help Parents Promote Growth of Their Retarded Child." *Social Work* 9 (October 1964).

Budner, Stanley et al. "The Minority Retardate: A Paradox in a Problem in Definition." *Social Service Review* 43 (June 1969).

Cobb, Henry. "The Attitude of the Retarded Person Towards Himself." In *Social Work and Mental Retardation*. Edited by Meyer Schreiber. New York: John Day Co., 1970.

Dickerson, Martha. *Social Work Practice With the Mentally Retarded*. New York: The Free Press, 1981.

Edgerton, Robert. *The Cloak of Competence: Stigma in the Lives of the Mentally Retarded*. Berkeley: University of California Press, 1969.

Goodman, David. "Parenting An Adult Mentally Retarded Offspring." *Smith College Studies in Social Work* 48 (June 1978).

Hersh, Alexander. "Casework with Parents of Retarded Children." *Social Work* 6 (April 1961).

_____. "Changes in Family Functioning Following Placement of a Retarded Child." *Social Work* 15 (July 1970).

Horejsi, Charles. "Developmental Disabilities: Opportunities for Social Workers." *Social Work* 24 (January 1979).

Jacobsen, R. Brooks, and Humphrey, Ruth. "Families in Crisis: Research and Theory in Child Mental Retardation." *Social Casework* 60 (December 1979).

Kaplan, Frances, and Fox, Elizabeth. "Siblings of the Retardate: An Adolescent Group Experience." *Community Mental Health Journal* 4 (December 1968).

Mandelbaum, Arthur, and Wheeler, Mary. "The Meaning of a Defective Child to Parents." *Social Casework* 41 (July 1960).

Mednick, Miriam. "Casework Service to the Mentally Retarded Child and His Parents." In *Differential Diagnosis and Treatment in Social Work*. Edited by Francis Turner. New York: The Free Press, 1968.

Noland, Robert, ed. *Counseling Parents of the Mentally Retarded: A Sourcebook*. Springfield, Ill.: Charles C Thomas, 1975.

Olshansky, Simon. "Chronic Sorrow: A Response to Having a Mentally Defective Child." *Social Casework* 43 (April 1962).

Oppenheimer, Sonja. "Early Identification of Mildly Retarded Children." *American Journal of Orthopsychiatry* 35 (October 1965).

Parnicky, Joseph, and Brown, Leonard. "'Introducing Institutionalized Retardates to the Community." *Social Work* 9 (January 1964).

Polansky, Norman et al. "Pseudo Stoicism in the Mothers of the Retarded." *Social Casework* 52 (December 1971).
Proctor, Enola. "New Directions for Work with Parents of Retarded Children." *Social Casework* 57 (April 1976).
Schild, Sylvia. "Counseling with Parents of Retarded Children Living at Home." *Social Work* 9 (January 1964). Also in *Differential Diagnosis and Treatment*. Edited by Francis Turner. New York: The Free Press, 1968, and 2d ed., 1976.
Schreiber, Meyer, ed. *Social Work and Mental Retardation*. New York: John Day Co., 1970.
Segal, Arthur. "Social Work with Mentally Retarded Adults in a Rehabilitation Setting." *Social Casework* 45 (December 1964).
Stone, Nellie. "Effecting Interdisciplinary Coordination in Clinical Services to the Mentally Retarded." *American Journal of Orthopsychiatry* 40 (October 1970).
Wolfensberger, Wolf et al. *Normalization: The Principle of Normalization in Human Services*. Toronto, Ontario: National Institute on Mental Retardation, 1972.

J. MENTAL HEALTH AND ILLNESS

Baldwin, Katherine. "Crisis Focused Casework in a Child Guidance Clinic." *Social Casework* 49 (January 1968).
Buxbaum, Carl. "Second Thoughts on Community Mental Health." *Social Work* 18 (May 1973).
Cain, Lillian. "Preparing a Psychotic Patient for Major Surgery." *Social Casework* 55 (July 1974).
Caplan, Gerald. *Principles of Preventive Psychiatry*. New York: Basic Books, 1964.
Christmas June, "Socio-Psychiatric Treatment of Disadvantaged Psychotic Adults." *American Journal of Orthopsychiatry* 37 (January 1967).
Cooper, Shirley. "The Swing to Community Mental Health." *Social Casework* 49 (May 1968).
Cumming, Elaine. "Three Issues Affecting Partnerships Among Mental Health Agencies." *Hospital and Community Psychiatry* 22 (February 1971).
Hilgard, Josephine, and Newman, Martha. "Anniversaries in Mental Illness." *Psychiatry* 22 (1959).

Jayaratne, Srinika. "Child Abusers as Parents and Children: A Review." *Social Work* 22 (January 1979).

Katz, Arthur, ed. *Community Mental Health: Issues for Social Work Practice and Education.* New York: Council for Social Work Education, 1979.

Kellam, Sheppard, and Schiff, Sheldon. "The Woodlawn Mental Health Center—A Community Mental Health Model." *Social Service Review* 40 (September 1966).

Kilguss, Anne. "Therapeutic Use of a Soap Opera Discussion Group With Psychiatric In-Patients." *Clinical Social Work Journal* 5 (Spring 1977).

Klein, D., and Lindemann, E. "Preventive Intervention in Individuals and Families." In *Prevention of Mental Disorders in Children.* Edited by G. Caplan. New York: Basic Books, 1961.

Kreisman, Dolores, and Virginia, Jay. "Family Response to the Mental Illness of a Relative: A Review of the Literature." *Schizophrenia Bulletin* 10 (Fall 1974).

Lourie, Norman. "Impact of Social Change on the Tasks of the Mental Health Professions." *American Journal of Orthopsychiatry* 35 (January 1965).

Margolis, Philip, and Favazzo Armado. "Mental Health and Illness." *Encyclopedia of Social Work.* 16th ed. New York: National Association of Social Workers, 1971.

Morrisey, James. *The Case for Family Care of the Mentally Ill.* New York: Behavioral Publications, 1967.

Poland, Phyllis. "The Community—New Psychiatric Treatment Center." In *Social Work Practice.* New York: National Association of Social Workers, Columbia University Press, 1963.

Portnoi, Tikvah et al. "Consultation by Participation in Child Psychiatry." *Social Casework* 54 (July 1973).

Rabkin, Julia. "Attitudes Toward Mental Illness." *Schizophrenia Bulletin* 10 (Fall 1974).

Scoles, Pascal, and Fine, Eric. "Aftercare and Rehabilitation in a Community Mental Health Center." *Social Work* 16 (July 1971).

Segal, Steven, and Baumohl, Jim. "Social Work Practice in Community Mental Health." *Social Work* 26 (January 1981).

Sturges, Jane. "Childrens' Reactions to Mental Illness in the Family." *Social Casework* 59 (November 1978).

Taylor Shirley, and Siegel, Norma. "Treating the Separation—Individuation Conflict." *Social Casework* 59 (June 1978).

93

Wallerstein, R. S. "The Challenge of the Community Mental Health Movement to Psychoanalysis." *American Journal of Psychiatry* 124 (February 1968).

Waring, Mary. "Averting Hospitalization for Adult Schizophrenics—A Search for Ameliorative Factors." *Social Work* 11 (October 1966).

Wolkon, George. "Effecting a Continuum of Care: An Exploration of the Crisis of Psychiatric Hospital Release." *Community Mental Health Journal* 4 (February 1968).

K. ALCOHOLISM AND OTHER DRUG ABUSE

Ackerman, Robert. *Children of Alcoholism*. Holme Beach, Fla.: Learning Publications Press, 1978.

Babcock, Marguerite, and Connor, Bernadette. "Sexism and Treatment of the Female Alcoholic: A Review." *Social Work* 26 (May 1981).

Bailey, Margaret. *Alcoholism and Family Casework*. New York: Community Council of Greater New York, 1968.

Blane, Howard. *The Personality of the Alcoholic*. New York: Harper and Row, 1968.

Blum, Eva. "Psychoanalytic Views of Alcoholism." *Quarterly Journal of Studies in Alcohol* 27 (June 1966).

———, and Blum, R. *Alcoholism: Modern Psychological Approaches to Treatment*. San Francisco: Jossey-Bass, 1972.

Brill, Leon. "Three Approaches to the Casework Treatment of Narcotic Addicts." *Social Work* 13 (April 1968).

———, and Winick, Charles. *The Yearbook of Substance Use and Abuse Vol. II*. New York: Human Sciences Press, 1980. See especially Part 2, Treatment; Brill, Leon. "The Treatment of Drug Abuse: Evolution of a Perspective," and Aprill, Floyd. "Methadone Treatment as a Crisis Precipitant."

Caroff, Phyllis; Lieberman, Florence; and Gottesfeld, Mary. "The Drug Problem: Treating Preaddictive Adolescents." *Social Casework* 51 (November 1970).

Chappel, J. N. "Modern Treatment of Drug Addiction: The Role of the Welfare Worker in Addict Rehabilitation." *Public Welfare* 28 (October 1970).

Cohen, Melvin, and Klein, Donald. "Drug Abuse in a Young Psychiatric Population." *American Journal of Orthopsychiatry* 40 (April 1970).

Cohen, Pauline, and Krause, Morton, eds. *Casework with Wives of Alcoholics.* New York: Family Service Association of America, 1971.

Cohen, Sidney, ed. *Drug Abuse and Alcoholism: Current Critical Issues.* New York: Haworth Press, 1981.

————. *The Substance Abuse Problems.* New York: Haworth Press, 1980.

Corrigan, Eileen. *Alcoholic Women in Treatment.* New York: Oxford University Press, 1980.

Curlee, John. "Depression and Alcoholism." *Bulletin of the Menninger Clinic* 36 (July 1972).

"Dimensions of Alcoholism Treatment." *Social Casework* 59 (January 1978).

Edwards, David. "The Family—A Therapeutic Model for the Treatment of Drug Addiction." *Clinical Social Work Journal* 1 (Spring 1973).

Eldred, Carolyn. "Comprehensive Treatment of Heroin—Addicted Mothers." *Social Casework* 55 (October 1974).

Ehline, David, and Tighe, Peggy. "Alcoholism: Early Identification and Intervention in the Social Service Agency." *Child Welfare* 56 (November 1977).

El-Gueblay, Nady, and Offord, David. "The Offspring of Alcoholics: A Cultural Review." *American Journal of Psychiatry* 134 (April 1977).

Fewell, Christine, and Bissell, Le Clair. "The Alcoholic Denial Syndrome: An Alcohol-Focused Approach." *Social Casework* 59 (January 1978).

Finlay, Donald. "Alcoholism: Problem in Interaction." *Social Work* 19 (July 1974).

————. "Anxiety and the Alocholic." *Social Work* 17 (November 1972).

————. "Effect of Role and Network Pressure on an Alcoholic's Approach to Treatment." *Social Casework* 47 (October 1966).

Hartman, Dora. "A Study of Drug-Taking Adolescents." *Psychoanalytic Study of the Child* 24 (1969).

Health and Social Work. Entire issue on alcohol problems. 4 (November 1979).

95

Hughes, Patrick. *Behind the Wall of Respect: Community Experiments in Heroin Addiction and Control*. Chicago: University of Chicago Press, 1977.

Kaufman, Edward, and Kaufman, Pauline. *Family Therapy of Drug and Alcohol Abuse*. New York: Gardner Press, 1979.

Klagsbrun, Micheline, and Davis, Donald. "Substance Abuse and Family Interaction." *Family Process* 16 (June 1977).

Koppel, Flora et al. "The Enabler: A Motivational Tool in Treating the Alcoholic." *Social Casework* 61 (November 1980).

Krimmel, Herman, ed. *Alcoholism: Challenge to Social Work Education*. New York: Council on Social Work Education, 1972.

Lingeman, Richard. *Drugs from A to Z*. New York: McGraw-Hill, 1968.

Maglin, Arthur. "Sex Role Differences in Heroin Addiction." *Social Casework* 55 (March 1974).

Mally, Mary. "A Study in Family Patterns of Alcoholic Marriages." *American Journal of Orthopsychiatry* 35 (March 1965).

McNamara, John. "The Disease Concept of Alcoholism: Its Therapeutic Value for the Alcoholic and His Wife." *Social Casework* 41 (November 1960).

Meeks, Donald, and Kelly, Colleen. "Family Therapy with the Families of Recovering Alcoholics." *Quarterly Journal of Studies in Alcohol* 31 (June 1970).

Miller, Peter; Stanford, Ann; and Hemphill, Diana. "A Social-learning Approach to Alcoholism Treatment." *Social Casework* 55 (May 1974).

Moffett, Arthur, and Chambers, Carl. "The Hidden Addiction." *Social Work* 15 (July 1970).

———— et al. "New Ways of Treating Addicts." *Social Work* 19 (July 1974).

Muller, Jolens. "Casework with the Family of the Alcoholic." *Social Work* 17 (September 1972).

Pertzoff, Liv. "An Alcoholism Program in an Industrial Society." *Smith College Studies in Social Work* 49 (June 1979).

Salmon, Robert. "An Analysis of Public Marijuana Policy." *Social Casework* 53 (January 1972).

Schacter, Burt. "Psychedelic Drug Use by Adolescents." *Social Work* 13 (July 1968).

Snyder, Veronica. "Cognitive Approaches in the Treatment of Alcoholism." *Social Casework* 56 (October 1975).

St. Pierre, Andre. "Motivating the Drug Addict in Treatment."
Social Work 16 (January 1971).
_____. "A Treatment Program for the Drug Dependent Patient."
Social Work 14 (April 1969).
Strayer, Robert. "The Social Worker's Role in Handling the
Resistance of the Alcoholic." In *Differential Diagnosis and
Treatment in Social Work*. Edited by Francis Turner. New York:
The Free Press, 1968, 2d ed., 1976.
Triana, Robert, and Hinkle, Lorraine. "Psychoanalytically Oriented
Therapy for the Alcoholic Patient." *Social Casework* 55 (May 1974).
Weinberg, Jon. "Counseling Recovering Alcoholics." *Social
Casework* 18 (July 1973). Also in Turner's *Differential Diagnosis
and Treatment*. (See entry under Strayer above.)
_____. "Inteview Techniques for Diagnosing Alcoholism." *Family
Medicine* 9 (March 1974).
Wilder, Herbert, and Kaplan, Eugene. "Drug Use in Adolescents."
Psychoanalytic Study of the Child 24 (1969).
Wood, Howard, and Duffy, Edward. "Psychological Factors in
Alcoholic Women." *American Journal of Psychiatry* 123
(September 1966).

L. FAMILY PLANNING

Bradshaw, Barbara et al. *Counseling on Family Planning and Human
Sexuality*. New York: Family Service Association of America, 1977.
Brieland, Donald. "Bioethical Issues in Family Planning." *Social
Work* 24 (November 1979).
Byrne, Donn. "A Pregnant Pause in the Sexual Revolution."
Psychology Today 11 (July 1977).
Demarest, Robert, and Scearra, John. *Conception, Birth and
Contraception*. New York: McGraw-Hill, 1969.
Evans, Jerome; Selstad, Georgiana; and Welcher, Wayne.
"Teen-agers: Fertility Control Behavior and Attitudes Before and
After Abortion, Childbearing or Negative Pregnancy Test." *Family
Planning Perspectives* 8 (July-August 1976).
Family Planning Perspectives. Family planning journal published
bimonthly by Planned Parenthood Federation of America under
the direction of its research and development division, The Alan
Guttmacher Institute, New York, New York.

———. Special section on morbidity, costs, and emotional impact related to abortion methods. 9 (November-December 1977).

Freeman, Ellen. "Influence of Personality Attributes on Abortion Experiences." *American Journal of Orthopsychiatry* 47 (July 1977).

Furie, Sidney. "Birth Control and the Lower-Class Unmarried Mother." *Social Work* 11 (January 1966).

Gorman, Joanna, ed. *The Social Worker and Family Planning*. Based on proceedings of 1969 Institute for Public Health Social Workers. Berkeley: University of California, 1970.

Gould, Ketayun. "Family Planning and Abortion Policy in the United States." *Social Service Review* 53 (September 1979).

Gray, Naomi. "Family Planning and Social Welfare's Responsibility." *Social Casework* 47 (October 1966).

Grunebaum, Henry, and Abernethy, Virginia. "Marital Decision Making as Applied to Family Planning." *Journal of Sex as Applied to Family Planning* 1 (Fall 1974).

Haselkorn, Florence, ed. *Family Planning: Readings and Case Material*. New York: Council on Social Work Education, 1971.

———. *Family Planning: The Role of Social Work, Perspectives in Social Work*. Garden City, New York: Adelphi University School of Social Work, 1968.

———. *Mothers-At-Risk, Perspectives in Social Work*. Garden City, New York: Adelphi University School of Social Work, 1966.

Group for the Advancement of Psychiatry. Report no. 86. *Humane Reproduction*. New York: Charles Scribner's Sons, 1973.

Kendall, Katherine, ed. *Population Dynamics and Family Planning: A New Responsibility for Social Work Education*. New York: Council on Social Work Education, 1971.

Lane, M. E. *Contraception for Adolescents*. Pamphlet 91351. New York: Planned Parenthood-World Population 1973.

Lipscomb, Nell. "Caseworker and Family Planning." *Social Casework* 50 (April 1969).

Manisoff, Miriam, ed. *Family Planning Training for Social Service*. New York: Planned Parenthood-World Population. 2d ed., rev. 1973.

Mendelson, June, and Domolky, Serena. "The Courts and Elective Abortions Under Medicaid." *Social Service Review* 54 (March 1980).

Meyer, Henry, and Stone, Judith. *Family Planning and the Practice of Social Workers*. Pamphlet 91488. New York: Planned Parenthood-World Population, 1974.

Norman, Alex. "Family Planning With Third-World Males." *Health and Social Work* 2 (August 1977).

Oettinger, Katherine, *Social Work in Action: An International Perspective on Population and Family Planning*. New York: International Association of Schools of Social Work, 1975.

Rothstein, Arden. "Abortion: A Dyadic Perspective." *American Journal of Orthopsychiatry* 47 (January 1977).

Russell, Betty, and Schild, Sylvia. "Pregnancy Counseling with College Women." *Social Casework* 57 (May 1976).

Scales, Peter. "The Context of Sex Education and the Reduction of Teenage Pregnancy." *Child Welfare* 58 (April 1979).

Silverman, Anna, and Silverman, Arnold. *The Case Against Having Children*. New York: David McKay, 1971.

Smith, Mary. "Birth Control and the Negro Woman." *Ebony* (March 1968). Reprinted by Planned Parenthood Federation of America. Pamphlet 967. New York: Planned Parenthood-World Population, 1968.

Srikantan, K. *The Family Planning Program in the Socioeconomic Context*. New York: Population Council, 1977.

Stanford, Helen. "The Caseworker, the Client and Family Planning." Pamphlet 971. New York: Planned Parenthood-World Population, 1968.

Varela, Alice, ed. *Family Planning*. New Brunswick, N.J.: The Graduate School of Social Work, Rutgers University, 1968.

Sung, Kyu-Taik. "Family Planning Services for Indigent Women and Girls." *Health and Social Work* 3 (November 1978).

Torres, Aida. "Organized Family Planning Services in the United States, 1968–1976." *Family Planning Perspectives* 10 (May-June 1978).

Vadies, Eugene, and Hale, Darryl. "Attitudes of Adolescent Males Toward Abortion, Contraception and Sexuality." *Social Work in Health Care* 3 (Winter 1977).

1. INFERTILITY

Debrovner, Charles, and Shubin-Stern, Roselle. "Sexual Problems Associated with Infertility." *Human Sexuality* 10 (March 1976).

Freedman, Ronald. *The Sociology of Human Fertility: An Annotated Bibliography*. New York: John Wiley and Sons, 1975.

Kaufman, Sherwin. A. *New Hope for the Childless Couple*. New York: Simon and Schuster, 1970.

Masters, William, and Johnson, Virginia. "Advice for Women Who Want to Have a Baby." *Redbook* (March 1975).
Menning, Barbara. "The Infertile Couple: A Plea for Advocacy." *Child Welfare* 54 (June 1975).
————. *Infertility*. Englewood Cliffs, N.J.: Prentice-Hall, 1977.
Rienne, Diane. "There's Always Adoption: The Infertility Problem." *Child Welfare* 56 (July 1977).

2. DECISION MAKING REGARDING PARENTHOOD AND NONPARENTHOOD

See related items under Out-of-Wedlock Pregnancy and Unwed Parenthood.

Chilman, Catherine. "Parent Satisfactions-Dissatisfactions and Their Correlates." *Social Service Review* 53 (June 1979).
Dils, Suzanne, and Smith, Larry. "Genetic Counseling: Implications for Social Work Practice." *Clinical Social Work Journal* 8 (Summer 1980).
Goodbody, Sandra. "The Psychosocial Implications of Voluntary Childlessness." *Social Casework* 58 (July 1977).
Hsia, Eward et al., eds. *Counseling in Genetics*. New York: Alan R. Less, 1979.
Kaminsky, Barbara, and Scheckter, Lorraine. "Abortion Counseling in a General Hospital." *Health and Social Work* 4 (May 1979).
Lott, Bernice. "Who Wants the Children?" *American Psychologist* 28 (1973).
Ory, Marcia. "The Decision to Parent or Not: Normative and Structural Components." *Journal of Marriage and the Family* 40 (August 1978).
Peck, Ellen. *The Baby Trap*. New York: Bernard Geis Associates, 1971.
Whelan, Elizabeth M. *A Baby . . . Maybe*. New York: The Bobbs-Merill Co., 1975.
Swigar, Mary; Quinlan, Donald; and Wexler, Sherry. "Abortion Applicants: Characteristics Distinguishing Dropouts Remaining Pregnant and Those Having Abortion." *American Journal of Public Health* 67 (February 1977).

M. OUT-OF-WEDLOCK PREGNANCY AND UNWED PARENTHOOD

See related items under Family Planning, especially under Decision Making Regarding Parenthood and Nonparenthood.

Anderson, Portia et al. "Brief Service to Unmarried Mothers." In *Brief and Intensive Casework with Unmarried Mothers*. New York: Child Welfare League of America and National Conference on Social Welfare, 1962.

Bemis, Judith et al. "The Teen-age Single Mother." *Child Welfare* 55 (May 1976).

Bernstein, Rose. "Are We Still Stereotyping the Unmarried Mother?" *Social Work* 5 (July 1960).

Blatt, Marianne. "Intensive Casework with the Unmarried Mother and Her First Pregnancy: Emphasis on Rehabilitation and Prevention of Recidivism." In *Brief and Intensive Casework with Unmarried Mothers*. New York: Child Welfare League of America and National Conference on Social Welfare, 1962.

Bracken, Michael; Klerman, Lorraine; and Bracken, Maryann. "Coping With Pregnancy—Resolution Among Never-Married Women." *American Journal of Orthopsychiatry* 48 (April 1978).

Byrne, Donn. "A Pregnant Pause in the Sexual Revolution." *Psychology Today* 11 (July 1977).

Caughlan, Jeanne. "Psychic Hazards of Unwed Paternity." *Socal Work* 5 (July 1960).

Chaskel, Ruth. "Changing Patterns of Services for Unmarried Parents." *Social Casework* 49 (January 1968).

Chesler, Joan, and Davis, Susan. "Problem Pregnancy and Abortion Counseling With Teenagers." *Social Casework* 61 (March 1980).

Chilman, Catherine. "Teenage Pregnancy: A Research Review." *Social Work* 24 (November 1979).

Deutsch, Helene. *The Psychology of Women*. New York: Grune and Stratton, 1945. See especially Chap. 10, "Unmarried Mothers."

Dukette, Rita, and Stevenson, Nicholas. "The Legal Rights of Unmarried Fathers: The Impact of Recent Court Decisions." *Social Service Review* 47 (March 1973).

Friedman, Helen. "Why Are They Keeping Their Babies?" *Social Work* 20:4 (July 1975).

Furstenberg, Frank, Jr. *Unplanned Parenthood: The Social Consequences of Teen-age Child Bearing.* New York: The Free Press, 1976.

Grow, Lucille. Today's Unmarried Mothers: The Choices Have Changed." *Child Welfare* 58 (June 1979).

Herzog, Elizabeth. "Unmarried Mothers: Some Questions to be Answered and Some Answers to be Questioned." *Child Welfare* 41 (October 1962).

Hildebrand, Catherine. "Casework with Different Kinds of Unwed Mothers." In *Perspectives on Services for Unmarried Mothers.* New York: Child Welfare League of America, 1964.

Kreech, Florence. "The Current Role and Services of Agencies for Unwed Parents and Their Children." *Child Welfare* 53 (May 1974).

_____. "A Residence for Mothers and Their Babies." *Child Welfare* 54 (September-October 1975).

Lewis, Richard. "The Unmarried Parent and Community Resources." *Child Welfare* 47 (December 1968).

Menders, Helen. "Single Fatherhood." *Social Work* 21 (July 1976).

Pannor, Reuben. *The Unmarried Father.* New York: Springer Publishing. 1971.

Papademetriou, Marguerite. "Use of a Group Technique with Unwed Mothers and Their Families." *Social Work* 16 (October 1971).

Perlman, Helen. "Unmarried Mothers". In *Social Work and Social Problems.* Edited by Nathan E. Cohen. New York: National Association of Social Workers, 1964.

Platts, Hal. "A Public Adoption Agency's Approach to Natural Fathers." *Child Welfare* 47 (November 1968).

Plionis, Betty. "Adolescent Pregnancy, A Review of the Literature." *Social Work* 20 (July 1975).

Reiner, Beatrice. "The Real World of the Teen-Aged Negro Mother." *Child Welfare* 47 (July 1968).

Russell, Betty, and Schild, Sylvia. "Pregnancy Counseling with College Women." *Social Casework* 57 (May 1976).

Signell, Karen. "Mental Health Consultation in the Field of Illegitimacy." *Social Work* 14 (April 1969).

Singer, Ann. "A Program for Young Mothers and Their Babies." *Social Casework* 52 (November 1971).

Strean, Herbert. "Reconsiderations in Casework Treatment of the Unmarried Mother." *Social Work* 13 (October 1968). Also in *Differential Diagnosis and Treatment in Social Work.* Edited by Francis Turner. New York: The Free Press, 1968, 2d ed., 1976.

Ullmann, Alice. "Social Work Service to Abortion Patients." *Social Casework* 53 (October 1972). Also in Turner's *Differential Diagnosis and Treatment*. (See entry under Strean above.)

Young, Alma et al. "Parental Influence on Pregnant Adolescents." *Social Work* 20 (September 1975).

Young, Leontine. *Out of Wedlock*. New York: McGraw-Hill, 1954.

N. OTHER SEXUAL ORIENTATIONS

Abbott, Sidney, and Love, Barbara. *Sappho Was A Right On Woman*. New York: Stein and Day, 1973.

Altman, Dennis, *Homosexual Oppression and Liberation*. New York: E. P. Dutton and Co., 1971.

Bailey, Roy, and Brake, Mike "Homosexuality: Sexual Needs and Social Problems." In *Radical Social Work*. New York: Pantheon Books, 1975.

Bates, John et al. "Intervention with Families of Gender-Disturbed Boys." *American Journal of Orthopsychiatry* 45 (January 1975).

Bell, Alan, and Weinberg, Martin. *Homosexualities: A Study of Diversity Among Men and Women*. New York: Simon and Shuster, 1978.

Berger, Raymond. "An Advocate Model for Intervention With Homosexuals." *Social Work* 22 (July 1977).

Bernstein, Barton. "Legal and Social Interface in Counseling Homosexual Clients." *Social Casework* 58 (January 1977).

Chesler, Phyllis. *Women and Madness*. New York: Avon Books/Doubleday, 1972. See especially Chap. 7.

Churchill, Wainwright, *Homosexual Behavior Among Males*. Englewood Cliffs, N.J.: Prentice-Hall, 1967.

deMonteflores, Carmen, and Schultz, Stephen. "Coming Out: Similarities and Differences for Lesbians and Gay Men." *Journal of Social Issues* 34 (Summer 1978).

Fisher, Peter. *The Gay Mystique: The Myth and Reality of Male Homosexuality*. New York: Stein and Day, 1972.

Franks, Violet, and Burtle, Vasanti, eds. *Women in Therapy*. New York: Brunner/Mazel, 1974.

Green, Richard. *Sexual Identity Conflict in Children and Adults*. New York: Basic Books, 1974.

Hall, Marny. "Lesbian Families: Cultural and Clinical Issues." *Social Work* 23 (September 1978).

Jay, Karla, and Young, Allen, eds. *Out of the Closet: Voices of Gay Liberation*. Moonachie, N.J.: Pyramid Publications, 1974.

Kwawer, Jay. "Transference and Countertransference in Homosexuality—Changing Psychoanalytic Views." *American Journal of Psychotherapy* 34 (January 1980).

Leader, Elaine. "Transsexualism: A Study of Cross-Gender Identity Disorder." *Clinical Social Work Journal* 3 (Fall 1975).

Levine, Candace. "Social Work with Transsexuals." *Social Casework* 59 (March 1978).

Lewis, Karen. "Children of Lesbians: Their Point of View." *Social Work* 25 (May 1980).

Lewis, Sasha. *Sunday's Woman: A Report on Lesbian Life Today*. Boston: Beacon Press, 1979.

Loewenstein, Sophie. "Understanding Lesbian Women." *Social Casework* 61 (January 1980).

Malyon, Alan. "The Homosexual Adolescent: Developmental Issues and Social Bias." *Child Welfare* 60 (May 1981).

Martin, Del, and Lyon, Phillis. *Lesbian Woman*. New York: Bantam Books, 1972.

Mitchell, Stephen. "Psychodynamics, Homosexuality, and the Question of Pathology." *Psychiatry* 41 (August 1978).

Moses, Alice. *Identity Management in Lesbian Women*. New York: Frederick A. Praeger, 1978.

Needham, Russell. "Casework Intervention with a Homosexual Adolescent." *Social Casework* 58 (July 1977).

Potter, Sandra, and Darty, Trudy. "Social Work and the Invisible Minority: An Exploration of Lesbianism." *Social Work* 26 (May 1981).

"Psychology and the Gay Community." *Journal of Social Issues*. Entire issue on gay topics. 34 (Summer 1978).

Silverstein Charles. *A Family Matter: A Parent's Guide to Homosexuality*. Highstown, N.J.: 1977.

Tripp, C. A. *The Homosexual Matrix*. New York: McGraw-Hill, 1975.

Weinberg, George. *Society and the Healthy Homosexual*. New York: Anchor Press/Doubleday, 1973.

Wolff, Charlotte. *Love Between Women*. New York: St. Martin's Press, 1971.

Woodman, Natalie, and Lenna, Harry. *Counseling With Gay Men and Women: A Guide for Facilitating Positive Life-Styles*. San Francisco: Jossey-Bass, 1980.

O. SEXUAL DEVIANCE

See related items under Children.

Brant, Renee, and Tisza, Veronica. "The Sexually Misused Child." *American Journal of Orthopsychiatry* 47 (January 1977).

Brown, Selma. "Clinical Illustrations of the Sexual Misuse of Girls." *Child Welfare* 58 (July-August 1979).

de Young, Mary. "Siblings of Oedipus: Brothers and Sisters of Incest Victims." *Child Welfare* 60 (September-October 1981).

Dietz, Christine, and Craft, John. "Family Dynamics of Incest: A New Perspective." *Social Casework* 61 (December 1980).

Ellis, Albert, and Brancale, R. *The Psychology of Sex Offenders.* Springfield, Ill.: Charles C Thomas, 1956.

Elwell, Mary. "Sexually Assaulted Children and Their Families." *Social Casework* 60 (April 1979).

F inkelhor., David. *Sexually Victimized Children.* New York: The Free Press, 1979.

Forward, Susan, and Buck, Craig. *Betrayal of Innocence: Incest and Its Devastation.* New York: Penguin Books, 1979.

Gagnon, John, and Simon, William, eds. *Sexual Deviance.* New York: Harper and Row, 1967.

Geiser, Robert. *Hidden Victims: The Sexual Abuse of Children.* Boston: Beacon Press, 1977.

Gentry, Charles. "Incestuous Abuse of Children: The Need for an Objective View." *Child Welfare* 57 (June 1978).

Hackett, Thomas. "Psychotherapy of Exhibitionists in a Court Clinic Setting." *Seminars in Psychiatry* 3 (August 1971).

Howell, Leisla. "Clinical and Research Impressions Regarding Murder and Sexually Perverse Crimes." *Psychotherapy and Psychosomatics* 21 (1972–73).

Justice, Blair, and Justice, Rita. *The Broken Taboo: Sex in the Family.* New York: Human Sciences Press, 1979.

Kenefick, Donald. *Conference Manual on Law Enforcement and the Sexual Offender: Law Medicine Institute.* Boston: Boston University, 1964.

Kreiger, Marilyn et al. "Problems in the Psychotherapy of Children With Histories of Incest." *American Journal of Psychotherapy* 34 (January 1980).

Lewis, Melvin, and Sarrel, Philip. "Some Psychological Aspects of Seduction, Incest, and Rape in Children." *Journal of the American Academy of Child Psychiatry* 8 (Fall 1969).

Misselman, Karin. *Incest: A Psychological Study of Causes and Effects With Treatment Recommendations.* San Francisco: Jossey-Bass, 1979.

Nasjleci, Maria. "Suffering in Silence: The Male Incest Victim." *Child Welfare* 59 (May 1980).

Peters, Joseph. "Children Who Are Victims of Sexual Assault and the Psychology of Offenders." *American Journal of Psychotherapy* 13 (July 1976).

Resnik, H. L. P. "Symposium: Treatment of Sexual Offenders." *Medical Aspects of Human Sexuality* 3 (August 1969).

Russell, Donald. "Emotional Aspects of Shoplifting." *Psychiatric Annals* 3 (May 1973).

———. "Symposium: Treatment of Sexual Offenders." *Medical Aspects of Human Sexuality* 3 (August 1969).

Schultz, LeRoy. "The Sexual Abuse of Children and Minors: A Bibliography." *Child Welfare* 58 (March 1979).

Shamroy, Jerilyn. "A Perspective on Childhood Sexual Abuse." *Social Work* 25 (March 1980).

Shelton, William. "A Study of Incest." *International Journal of Offender Therapy and Comparative Criminology* 19 (1975).

Silver, Steven. "Outpatient Treatment for Sexual Offenders." *Social Work* 21 (March 1976).

Spencer, Joyce. "Father-Daughter Incest: A Clinical View From the Corrections Field." *Child Welfare* 57 (November 1978).

Summit, Roland, and Kryso, JoAnn. "Sexual Abuse of Children: A Clinical Spectrum." *American Journal of Orthopsychiatry* 48 (April 1978).

Wax, Douglas, and Haddox, Victor. "Enuresis, Fire Setting and Animal Cruelty in Male Adolescent Delinquents: A Triad Predictive of Violent Behavior." *Journal of Psychiatry and Law* 2 (Spring 1974).

1. RAPE

Abarbanel, Gail. "Helping Victims of Rape." *Social Work* 21 (November 1976).

Amir, Menachem. *Patterns of Forcible Rape.* Chicago: University of Chicago Press, 1971.

Brownmiller, Susan. *Against Our Will: Men, Women, and Rape*. New York: Bantam Books, 1976.

Burgess, Ann, and Holmstrom, Lynda. "Rape Trauma Syndrome." In *Differential Diagnosis and Treatment In Social Work*. Edited by Francis Turner. New York: The Free Press, 1968, 2d ed., 1976.

———. "The Rape Victim in the Emergency Ward." *American Journal of Nursing* 73 (October 1973).

Cohen, Murray et al. "The Psychology of Rapists." *Seminars in Psychiatry* 3 (August 1971).

Fox, Sandra, and Scherl, Donald. "Crisis Intervention with Rape Victim." *Social Work* 17 (January 1972).

Groth, A. Nicholas, and Burgess, Ann. "Rape: A Sexual Deviation." *American Journal of Orthopsychiatry* 47 (July 1977).

Hilberman, Elaine. *The Rape Victim*. Washington, D.C.: American Psychiatric Association, 1976.

Kemmer, Elizabeth. *Rape and Rape-Related Issues: An Annotated Bibliography*. New York: Garland STPM Press, 1977.

Kilpatrick, Dean; Veronen, Lois; and Resnick, Patricia. "The Aftermath of Rape: Recent Empirical Findings." *American Journal of Orthosychiatry* 49 (October 1979).

Libow, Judith, and Doty, David. "An Exploratory Approach to Self-Blame and Self-Derogation by Rape Victims." *American Journal of Orthopsychiatry* 49 (October 1979).

McCombie, Sharon. "Characteristics of Rape Victims Seen in Crisis Intervention." *Smith College Studies in Social Work* 46 (April 1976).

MacDonald, John. *Rape: Offenders and Their Victims*. Springfield, Ill.: Charles C Thomas, 1971.

Notman, Malkah, and Nadelson, Carol. "The Rape Victim: Psychodynamic Considerations." *American Journal of Psychiatry* 133 (April 1976).

Schultz, LeRoy. *Rape Victimology*. Springfield, Ill.: Charles C Thomas, 1975.

Silverman, Daniel. "Sharing the Crisis of Rape: Counseling the Mates and Families of Victims." *American Journal of Orthopsychiatry* 48 (January 1978).

Sutherland, Sandra, and Scherl, Donald. "Crisis Intervention With Victims of Rape." *Social Work* 17 (January 1972).

———. "Patterns of Response Among Victims of Rape." *American Journal of Orthopsychiatry* 40 (April 1970).

P. CORRECTIONS

Blumberg, Marvin. "The Abusing Mother—Criminal Psychopath or Victim of Circumstances." *American Journal of Psychotherapy* 34 (July 1980).

Borgman, Robert. "Diversion of Law Violators to Mental Health Facilities." *Social Casework* 56 (July 1975).

Burnett, Bruce; Carr, John; Sinapi, John; and Taylor, Roy. "Police and Social Workers in a Community Outreach Program." *Social Casework* 57 (January 1976).

Chaiklin, Harris, and Kelly, Gerard. "The Domestic Relations Offender." *Social Service Review* 49 (March 1975).

Emerson, R. M. *Judging Delinquents: Content and Process in a Juvenile Court*. Chicago: Aldine Publishing, 1968.

Feild, Hubert, and Barnett, Nona. "Forcible Rape: An Updated Bibliography." *Journal of Criminal Law and Criminology* 68 (March 1977).

Goffman, Erving. *Asylums: Essays on the Social Situations of Mental Patients and Other Inmates*. New York: Doubleday, 1961.

Gutierres, Sara, and Reich, John. "A Developmental Perspective on Runaway Behavior: Its Relationship to Child Abuse." *Child Welfare* 60 (February 1981).

Handler, Ellen. "Family Surrogates as Correctional Strategy." *Social Service Review* 48 (December 1974).

Harper, Mary. "Courts, Doctors, and Delinquents: An Inquiry Into the Uses of Psychiatry in Youth Corrections." *Smith College Studies in Social Work* 44 (June 1974).

Heinz, Joe; Galaway, Burt; and Hudson, Joe. "Restitution or Parole: A Follow-up Study of Adult Offenders." *Social Service Review* 50 (March 1976).

Konopka, Gisela. "Our Outcast Youth." *Social Work* 15 (March 1970).

Lystad, Mary. "Violence at Home: A Review of the Literature." *American Journal of Orthopsychiatry* 45 (April 1975).

Martinez, Anthony. "Social Workers, Evidentiary Testimony and the Courts." *Journal of Education for Social Work* 16 (Winter 1980).

Michaels, Rhoda, and Treger, Harvey. "Social Work in Police Departments." *Social Work* 18 (September 1973).

Miller, Jill. "Teaching Law and Legal Skills to Social Workers." *Journal of Education for Social Work* 16 (Fall 1980).

National Association of Social Workers. *Law and Social Work*. Washington, D.C.: National Association of Social Workers, 1973.

Palmer, Ted. "Matching Worker and Client in Corrections." *Social Work* 18 (March 1973).

Peoples, Edward, ed. *Readings in Correctional Casework and Counseling*. Santa Monica, Calif.: Goodyear Publishing, 1975.

Pierce, L. "Rehabilitation in Corrections: A Reassessment." *Federal Probation* 38 (January 1974).

Raymond, Frank. "To Punish or To Treat." *Social Work* 19 (May 1974).

Reiner, Beatrice, and Kaufman, Irving. *Character Disorders in Parents of Delinquents*. New York: Family Service Association of America, 1959.

Rolde, Edward et al. "A Law Enforcement Training Program in a Mental Health Catchment Area." *American Journal of Psychiatry* 130 (September 1973).

Ross, Bernard, and Shireman, Charles, eds. *Social Work Practice and Social Justice*. Washington, D.C.: National Association of Social Workers, 1973.

Russell, D. H. "Emotional Aspects of Shoplifting." *Psychiatric Annals* 3 (May 1973).

Schrier, Carol. "Child Abuse—An Illness or a Crime?" *Child Welfare* 58 (April 1979).

Schultz, LeRoy. "The Child Sex Victim: Social, Psychological and Legal Perspectives." *Child Welfare* 52 (March 1973).

Senna, Joseph. "Social Workers in Public Defender Programs." *Social Work* 20 (July 1975).

Shireman, Charles. "The Justice System and the Practice of Social Work." *Social Work* 19 (September 1974).

Spencer, Joyce. "Father-Daughter Incest: A Clinical View from the Field." *Child Welfare* 57 (November 1978).

Strean, Herbert. "A Psychosocial View of Social Deviance." *Clinical Social Work Journal* 4 (Fall 1976).

Studt, Elliot. *A Conceptual Approach to Teaching Materials: Illustrations from the Field of Corrections*. New York: Council on Social Work Education, 1965.

————. "Worker-Client Authority Relationships in Social Work." *Social Work* 4 (January 1959).

Treger, Harvey, "Police—Social Work Cooperation: Problems and Issues." *Social Casework* 62 (September 1981).

Webb, Allen, and Riley, Patrick. "Effectiveness of Casework with Young Female Probationers." *Social Casework* 51 (November 1970).

Weiner, Ronald. "The Criminal Justice System at the Breaking Point." *Social Work* 20 (November 1975).

Weisman, Irving. "Offender Status, Role Behavior, and Treatment Considerations." *Social Casework* 48 (July 1967).

Wax, Douglas, and Haddox, Victor. "Enuresis, Fire Setting, and Animal Cruelty in Male Adolescent Delinquents: A Trend Predictive of Violent Behavior." *Journal of Psychiatry and Law* 2 (Spring 1974).

Whiskin, Frederick. "Enforced Psychotherapy." *International Journal of Offender Therapy* 13 (1969).

Wright, David. *The Social Worker and the Courts*. Exeter, N.H.: Educational Books, 1979.

Yelaja, Shanker. *Authority and Social Work: Concept and Use*. Toronto: University of Toronto Press, 1971.

IV. Evaluation

A. GENERAL PRINCIPLES

Barth, Richard. "Education for Practice-Research: Toward a
Reorientation." *Journal of Education for Social Work* 17 (Spring
1981).
Beck, Dorothy Fahs, and Jones, Mary Ann. *How to Conduct a Client
Follow-up Study.* New York: Family Service Association of
America, 1974.
————. "A New Look at Clientele and Services of Family Agencies."
Social Casework 55 (December 1974).
Bernard, Sydney. "Why Service Delivery Programs Fail." *Social
Work* 20 (May 1975).
Bloom, Martin, and Gordon, William. "Measurement Through
Practice." *Journal of Education for Soical Work* 14 (Winter 1978).
Chernitsky, Roslyn, and Lurie, Abraham. "Developing A Quality
Assurance Program." *Health and Social Work* 1 (February 1976).
Conte, Jon, and Levy, Rona. "Problems and Issues in Implementing
the Clinical-Research Model of Practice in Educational and Clinical
Settings." *Journal of Education for Social Work* 16 (Fall 1980).
Fanshel, David, ed. *Future of Social Work Research, Selected
Papers.* New York: National Association of Social Workers, 1980.
Gambrill, Eileen, and Barth, Richard. "Single-Case Study Designs
Revisited." *Social Work Research and Abstracts* 16 (Fall 1980).
Gingerich, Wallace. "Procedure for Evaluating Clinical Practice."
Health and Social Work 4 (May 1979).
Haselkorn, Florence. "Accountability in Clinical Practice." *Social
Casework* 59 (June 1978).
Herstein, Norman. "The Challenge of Evaluation in Residential
Treatment." *Child Welfare* 54 (March 1975).
Ho, Man Keung. "Evaluation: A Means of Treatment." *Social Work*
21:1 (January 1976).
Hollis, Florence. "Evaluation: Clinical Results and Research
Methodology." *Clinical Social Work Journal* 4 (Fall 1976).
Howe, Michael. "Casework Self-Evaluation: A Single Subject
Approach." *Social Service Review* 48 (March 1974).
Kagle, Jill. "Evaluating Social Work Practice." *Social Work* 24 (July
1979).

McCurdy, William. *Program Evaluation: A Conceptual Tool Kit for Human Service Delivery Managers.* New York: Family Service Association of America, 1979.

Magura, Stephen, and Moses, Beth. "Outcome Measurement in Child Welfare." *Child Welfare* 59 (December 1980).

Mayer, Morris. "Program Evaluation As a Part of Clinical Practice: An Administrator's Position." *Child Welfare* 54 (June 1975).

Nelsen, Judith. "Issues in Single-Subject Research for Nonbehaviorists." *Social Work Research and Abstracts* 17 (Summer 1981).

Newman, Edward and Turem, Jerry. "The Crisis of Accountability." *Social Work* 19 (January 1974).

Rosenberg, Marvin, and Brody, Ralph. "The Threat or Challenge of Accountability." *Social Work* 19 (May 1974).

Rothman,, Jack. *Social R and D: Research and Development in the Human Services.* Englewood Cliffs, N.J.: Prentice-Hall, 1980.

Schoech, Dick, and Arangio, Tony. "Computers in the Human Services." *Social Work* 24 (March 1979).

Tripodi, Tony. *Research Trechniques for Clinical Social Workers.* New York: Columbia University Press, 1980.

Tropp, Emanuel. "Expectation, Performance, and Accountability." *Social Work* 19 (March 1974).

Watson, Kenneth. "Differential Supervision." *Social Work* 18 (November 1973).

Weatherley, Richard et al. "Accountability of Social Service Workers at the Front Line." *Social Service Review* 54 (December 1980).

Wechsler, Henry; Reinherz, Helen; and Dobbin, Donald. *Social Work Research in the Human Services.* New York: Human Sciences Press, 1981.

Weiss, Carol. "Alternative Models of Program Evaluation." *Social Work* 19 (November 1974).

B. SOCIAL RESEARCH DEVELOPMENTS IN CASEWORK PRACTICE

Beck, Dorothy Fahs. "Research Findings on the Outcomes of Marital Counseling." *Social Casework* 56 (January 1975).

_____, and Jones, Mary Ann. *Progress on Family Problems: A Nationwide Study of Clients' and Counselors' Views on Family Agency Services.* New York: Family Service Association of America, 1973.

Berelman, William, and Steiner, Thomas. "The Execution and Evaluation of a Delinquency Prevention Program." *Social Problems* 14 (Spring 1967).

Berg, Lawrence; Cohen, Stephen; and Reid, William. "Knowledge for Social Work Roles in Community Mental Health: Findings of Empirical Research." *Journal of Education for Social Work* 14 (September 1978).

Epstein, Laura. *Helping People: Task-Centered Approach*. St. Louis, Mo.: C. V. Mosby, 1980.

Fischer, Joel. "Is Casework Effective? A Review." *Social Work* 18 (January 1973).

Fraiberg, Selma. "The Muse in the Kitchen: A Case Study in Clinical Research." *Smith College Studies in Social Work* 40 (February 1970).

Grob, Mollie, and Singer, Judith. *Adolescent Patients in Transition*. New York: Behavioral Publications, 1974.

Gurman, Alan. "The Efficacy of Therapeutic Inverventions in Social Work: A Critical Re-evaluation." *Journal of Health and Social Behavior* 15 (June 1974).

Hollis, Florence. *Casework: A Psychosocial Therapy*. 2d ed. New York: Random House, 1972. See especially Chap. 10, "Studying and Working with the Typology."

_____. "Evaluation: Clinical Results and Research Methodology. An Essay Review." *Clinical Social Work Journal* 4 (Fall 1976).

Jones, Joan, and McNeely, R. "Mothers Who Neglect and Those Who Do Not: A Comparative Study." *Social Casework* 61 (November 1980).

Krider, James. "A Cost Analysis Study." *Social Casework* 56 (February 1975).

Leventhal, Theodore, and Weinberger, Gerald. "The Evaluation of a Large-Scale Brief Therapy Program for Children." *American Journal of Orthopsychiatry* 45 (January 1975).

Maas, Henry, ed. *Research in the Social Services: A Five-Year Review*. New York: National Association of Social Workers, 1971.

_____. *Social Service Research: Reviews of Studies*. New York: NASW Research Series, 1981.

_____, and Kuypers, Joseph. *From Thirty To Seventy*. San Francisco: Jossey-Bass, 1974.

Maluccio, Anthony. "Perspectives of Social Workers and Clients on Treatment Outcome." *Social Casework* 60 (July 1979).

113

Mayer, John, and Timms, Noel. *The Client Speaks: Working Class Impressions of Casework*. New York: Atherton Press, 1970.

Meyer, Henry; Borgata, Edgar; and Jones, Wyatt. *Girls of Vocational High: An Experiment in Social Work Intervention*. New York: Russell Sage Foundation, 1965.

Mullen, Edwards, and Dumpson, James, eds. *Evaluation of Social Work Intervention*. San Francisco: Jossey-Bass, 1972.

Parad, Howard, and Parad, Libbie. "Study of Crisis-Oriented Planned Short-Term Treatment: Part I." *Social Casework* 49 (June 1968).

———. "Study of Crisis-Oriented Planned Short-Term Treatment: Part II." *Social Casework* 49 (July 1968).

Pharis, Mary. "Ten Reasons Why I Am Not Bothered by Outcome Studies Which Claim to Show Psychotherapy is Ineffective." *Clinical Social Work Journal* 4 (Spring 1976).

Reid, William. "The Implications of Research for the Goals of Casework." *Smith College Studies in Social Work* 40 (February 1970).

———, and Epstein, Laura. *Task-Centered Casework*. New York: Columbia University Press, 1972.

———, and Shapiro, Barbara. "Client Reactions to Advice." *Social Service Review* 43 (June 1969).

———, and Shyne, Anne. *Brief and Extended Casework* New York: Columbia University Press, 1969.

Riley, Patrick. "Practice Changes Based on Research Findings." *Social Casework* 56 (April 1975).

Ripple, Lilian. *Motivation, Capacity and Opportunity: Studies in Casework Theory and Practice*. Chicago: University of Chicago, 1964.

Schwartz, Edward, and Sample, William. *The Midway Office: An Experiment in the Organization of Work Groups*. New York: National Association of Social Workers, 1972.

Segal, Steven. "Research on the Outcome of Social Work Intervention: A Review of the Literature." *Journal of Health and Social Behavior* 13 (March 1972).

Wallace, David. "The Chemung County Evaluation of Casework Services to Dependent Multi-Problems Families." *Social Service Review* 41 (December 1967).

Wood, Katherine. "Casework Effectiveness: A New Look at the Research Evidence." *Social Work* 23 (November 1978).

V. Additional Frames of Reference

See Turner, Francis, ed. *Social Work Treatment:* Interlocking Theoretical Approaches: New York: The Free Press, 2d ed., 1979, for a discussion of a variety of frames of reference.

A. BEHAVIOR MODIFICATION

Ayllon, Teodoro, and Azrin, Nathan. *The Token Economy: A Motivation System for Therapy Rehabilitation.* New York: Appleton-Century-Crofts, 1968.

Bruck, Max. "Behavior Modification Theory and Practice: A Critical Review." *Social Work* 13 (April 1968).

Child Welfare. Entire issue on behavior modification. 52 (October 1973).

Fisher, Phyllis. "Traditional Behavior Therapy—Competition or Collaboration?" *Social Casework* 54 (November 1973).

Franks, Cyril, ed. *Behavior Therapy: Appraisal and Status.* New York: McGraw-Hill, 1969.

Gambrill, Eileen. *Behavior Modification: Handbook of Assessment, Intervention, and Evaluation.* San Francisco: Jossey-Bass, 1977.

Hersen, Michel; Eisler, R.; and Miller, P. *Progress in Behavior Modification.* New York: Academic Press, 1976.

Jehu, Derek et al. *Behavior Modification in Social Work.* London: John Wiley and Sons, 1972.

Kanfer, Frederick, and Phillips, Jean. *Principles of Behavioral Analysis.* New York: John Wiley and Sons, 1970.

Lazarus, Arnold. *Behavior Therapy and Beyond.* New York: McGraw-Hill, 1971.

_____. "Has Behavior Therapy Outlived Its Usefulness?" *American Psychologist* 32 (July 1977).

McBeath, Marcia. "Helping Children by Changing their Behavior." *Child Welfare* 52 (February 1973).

Martin, Reed. *Legal Challenges to Behavior Modification: Trends in Schools, Corrections, and Mental Health.* Champaign, Ill.: Research Press, 1975.

Mehrabian, Albert. *Basic Behavior Modification.* New York: Human Sciences Press, 1978.

Meyer, V., and Chesser, E. *Behavior Therapy in Clinical Psychiatry*.
New York: Science House, 1970.
Rubin, Richard, ed. *Advances in Behavior Therapy*. New York:
Academic Press, 1972.
Saleebey, Dennis. "A Proposal to Merge Humanist and Behaviorist
Perspectives." *Social Casework* 58 (October 1975).
Schinke, Steven, ed. *Behavioral Methods in Social Welfare: Helping
Children, Adults, and Families in Community Settings*. New York:
Aldine Publishing Co., 1980.
Schwartz, Arthur. "Behaviorism and Psychodynamics." *Child
Welfare* 56 (June 1977).
Strean, Herbert. "Psychoanalytically Oriented Casework vs.
Behavior Modification Therapy." *Clinical Social Work Journal* 1
(Fall 1973).
Stuart, Richard. "Applications of Behavior Theory to Social
Casework." In *The Socio-Behavioral Approach and Applications to
Social Work*. Edited by E. Thomas. New York: Council on Social
Work Education, 1967.
_____. "Behavior Modification: A Technology of Social Change." In
Social Work Treatment: Interlocking Theoretical Approaches.
Edited by Francis Turner. New York: The Free Press, 1974.
Thomas, Edwin. *Behavior Modification Procedure: A Sourcebook*.
New York: Aldine Publishing, 1974.
_____, ed. *The Socio-Behavioral Approach and Applications to
Social Work*. New York: Council on Social Work Education, 1967.
Wadsworth, H. G. "Social Conditioning: Casework in a School
Setting." *Social Casework* 52 (January 1971).
Watson, David, and Thorp, Roland. *Self-Directed Behavior*.
Monterey, Calif.: Brooks/Cole, 1972.
Wetzel, R., and Tharp, R. *Behavior Modification in the Natural
Environment*. New York: Academic Press, 1969.
Wodarski, John, and Bagarozzi, Dennis. *Behavior Social Work*. New
York: Human Sciences Press, 1979.
Yates, A. *Theory and Practice in Behavior Therapy*. New York: John
Wiley and Sons, 1975.

B. GENERAL SYSTEMS THEORY

Chin, Robert. "The Utility of Systems Models and Developmental Models for Practitioners." In *The Planning and Change*. Edited by Warren Bennis, Kenneth Benne, and Robert Chin. New York: Holt, Rinehart, and Winston, 1968.

"General Systems Theory and Psychiatry." *American Handbook of Psychiatry: Vol. III*. New York: Basic Books, 1966.

Germain, Carel. "General Systems Theory and Ego Psychology: An Ecological Perspective." *Social Service Review* 52 (December 1978).

_____. "Social Study: Past and Future." *Social Casework* 49 (July 1968).

Gray, William; Duhl, Fred; and Rizzo, Nick, eds. *General Systems Theory and Psychiatry*. Boston: Little, Brown and Co., 1969.

Hartman, Ann. "To Think About the Unthinkable." *Social Casework* 51 (October 1970).

Hearn, Gordon, ed. *The General Systems Approach: Contribution Toward an Holistic Conception of Social Work*. New York: Council on Social Work Education, 1969.

Hoffman, Lynn, and Long, Florence. "A Systems Dilemma." *Family Process* 8 (September 1969).

Janchill, Mary. "Systems Concepts in Casework Theory and Practice." *Social Casework* 50 (February 1969).

Mailick, Mildred. "A Situational Perspective in Casework Theory." *Social Casework* 58 (July 1977).

Miller, J. *Living Systems*. New York: McGraw-Hill, 1978.

Nelsen, Judith. "Uses of Systems Theory in Casework I and II: A Proposal." *Journal of Education for Social Work* 8 (Fall 1972).

Rubin, Gerald. "General Systems Theory: An Organismic Conception for Teaching Modalities of Social Work Intervention." *Smith College Studies in Social Work* 43 (June 1973).

Siporin, Max. *An Introduction to Social Work Practice*. New York: Macmillan, 1975.

Spiegel, John. *Transactions: The Interplay Between Individual, Family and Society*. New York: Science House, 1971.

Von Bertalanffy, Ludwig. *General Systems Theory: Foundations, Development, Applications*. New York: George Braziller, 1968.

C. TRANSACTIONAL ANALYSIS

Barnes, Graham, ed. *Transactional Analysis After Eric Berne*. New York: Harpers College Press, 1977.

Berne, Eric. *Games People Play*. New York: Grove Press, 1964.

————. *Transactional Analysis in Psychotherapy*. Palo Alto, Calif.: Science and Behavior Books, 1970.

————. *"What Do You Say After You Say Hello?"* New York: Grove Press, 1972.

Brechenser, Donn. "Brief Psychotherapy Using Transactional Analysis." *Social Casework* 53 (March 1972).

Edwards, David. "The Family—A Therapeutic Model for the Treatment of Drug Addiction." *Clinical Social Work Journal* 1 (Spring 1973).

Goulding, Robert, and Goulding, Mary. "Injunctions, Decisions and Redecisions." *Transactional Analysis Journal* 6 (January 1976).

Harris, Thomas. *I'm OK—You're OK: A Practical Guide to Transactional Analysis*. New York: Harper and Row, 1967.

James, Muriel, and Jongeward, Dorothy. *Born to Win: Transactional Analysis with Gestalt Experiments*. Reading, Mass.: Addison Wesley, 1971.

Kahler, Taibi, and Capers, Hedges. "The Miniscript." *Transactional Analysis Journal* 4 (January 1974).

Schiff, Jacqui. *All My Children*. New York: Evans Publishing, 1970.

Thomas, M. Duane, and Mornson, Thomas. "Interdisciplinary Team Communications: TA as a Tool." *Clinical Social Work Journal* 5 (Summer 1977).

Steiner, Claude, *Scripts People Live*. New York: Grove Press, 1974.

Woollams, Stanley; Brown, Michael; and Huige, Kristyn. *Transactional Analysis in Brief*. Ann Arbor, Mich.: Huron Valley Institute, 1974.

D. NEO-FREUDIAN THERAPIES

Adler, Alfred. *The Individual Psychology of Alfred Adler*. Edited and annotated by Heinz L. and Rowena Ansbacher. New York: Basic Books, 1956.

Fromm, Erich. *Escape From Freedom*. New York: Farrar and Rinehart, 1941.

_____. *Heart of Man*. New York: Harper and Row, 1964.
Horney, Karen. *The Neurotic Personality of Our Time*. New York: W. W. Norton and Co., 1937.
_____. *New Ways in Psychoanalysis*. New York: W. W. Norton and Co., 1939.
Jung, Carl. *Modern Man in Search of a Soul*. New York: Harcourt Brace, 1934.
_____. *On the Nature of the Psyche*. Princeton, N.J.: Bollingen Series, 1969.
Lowen, Alexander. *The Betrayal of the Body*. New York: Macmillan and Company, 1970.
_____. *Depression and the Body*. New York: Coward, McCann and Geoghegan, 1972.
Rank, Otto. *Beyond Psychology*. New York: Dover, 1958.
_____. *Will Therapy and Truth and Reality*. New York: Knopf, 1945.
Reich, Wilhelm. *Character Analysis*. New York: Noonday Press, 1949.
Sullivan, Harry Stack. *The Interpersonal Theory of Psychiatry*. New York: W. W. Norton and Co., 1953.
_____. *The Psychiatric Interview*. New York: W. W. Norton and Co., 1954.

E. HUMANISTIC THERAPIES

1. EXISTENTIAL

Bradford, Kirk. *Existentialism and Casework*. Jericho, N.Y.: Exposition Press, 1969.
Edwards, David. *Existential Psychotherapy: The Process of Caring*. New York: Gardner Press, 1981.
Krill, Donald. "Existential Psychotherapy and the Problem of Anomie." *Social Work* 14 (April 1969).
_____. *Existential Social Work*. New York: The Free Press, 1978.
Laing, R. D. *Politics of Experience*. New York: Ballantine Books, 1967.
_____. *Sanity, Madness and the Family*. New York: Basic Books, 1971.

May, Rollo, ed. *Existential Psychology*. New York: Random House, 1961.

————. *Psychology and the Human Dilemma*. Princeton, N.J.: Van Nostrand, 1967.

Moustakas, Clark, ed. *The Child's Discovery of Himself*. New York: Ballantine Books, 1972.

Sartre, Jean Paul. *Existential Psychoanalysis*. New York: Philosophical Library, 1953.

Sinsheimer, Robert. "The Existential Casework Relationship." *Social Casework* 50 (February 1969).

Stretch, John. "Existentialism: A Proposed Philosophical Orientation for Social Work." *Social Work* 12 (October 1967).

Yalom, Irvin. *Existential Psychotherapy*. New York: Basic Books, 1980.

2. GESTALT

Fagan, Joan, and Shepherd, Irma, eds. *Gestalt Therapy Now: Theory, Techniques, Applications*. Palo Alto, Calif.: Science and Behavior Books, 1970.

Hale, B. John. "Gestalt Techniques in Marriage Counseling." *Social Casework* 59 (July 1978).

Hatcher, Chris, and Himelstein, Philip, eds. *Handbook of Gestalt Therapy*. New York: Jason Aronson, 1976.

Paul, Lyndell. "The Relevance of Gestalt Therapy for Social Work." *Clinical Social Work Journal* 1 (Summer 1973).

Passons, William. *Gestalt Approaches in Counseling*. New York: Holt, Rinehart and Winston, 1975.

Perls, Frederick. *The Gestalt Approach and Eye Witness to Therapy*. Palo Alto, Calif.: Science and Behavior Books, 1973.

————. *Gestalt Therapy Verbatim*. Moab, Utah: Real People Press, 1969.

————. *Legacy From Fritz*. Palo Alto, Calif.: Science and Behavior Books, 1975.

————; Hefferline, R.; and Goodman, P. *Gestalt Therapy: Excitement and Growth in the Human Personality*. New York: Dell Press, 1965.

Polster, Irving, and Polster, Miriam. *Gestalt Therapy: Integrated Contours of Theory and Practice*. New York: Brunner/Mazel, 1973.

120

Scanlon, Pauline. "A Gestalt Approach to Insight-Oriented Treatment." *Social Casework* 61 (September 1980).
Smith, E., ed. *The Growing Edge of Gestalt Therapy*. New York: Brunner/Mazel, 1976.
Tobin, Stephan. "Saying Good-bye to Gestalt Therapy." *Psychotherapy: Theory, Research and Practice* 8 (Summer 1971).
Zinker, Joseph. *Creative Process in Gestalt Therapy*. New York: Brunner/Mazel, 1977.

3. REALITY (COGNITIVE)

Beck, Aaron. *Cognitive Therapy and the Emotional Disorders*. New York: International Universities Press, 1976.
Bassin, Alexander; Bratter, Thomas; and Rachin, Richard. *The Reality Therapy Reader*. New York: Harper and Row, 1976.
Berlin, Sharon. "A Cognitive-Learning Perspective for Social Work." *Social Service Review* 54 (December 1980).
Ellis, Albert. *Reason and Emotion in Psychotherapy*. New York: Lyle Stuart, 1962.
Glasser, William. *Reality Therapy: A New Approach to Psychiatry*. New York: Harper and Row, 1965.
Werner, Harold. *New Understandings of Human Behavior*. New York: Association Press, 1970.
———. *A Rational Approach to Social Casework*. New York: Association Press, 1965.

4. SELF (CLIENT-CENTERED)

Hart, Joseph, and Tomlinson, Tommy, eds. *New Directions in Client-Centered Therapy*. Boston: Houghton Mifflin, 1970.
Maslow, Abraham. *Motivation and Personality*, 2d ed. New York: Harper and Row, 1970.
———. *Toward a Psychology of Being*. New York: Van Nostrand and Co., 1962.
Ornstein, Robert. *The Psychology of Consciousness*. San Francisco: W. H. Freeman and Co., 1972.
Rogers, Carl. *Carl Rogers on Personal Power*. New York: Delacorte Press, 1977.

_____. *Client-Centered Therapy*. Boston: Houghton Mifflin, 1951.
_____. *Counseling and Psychotherapy*. Boston: Houghton, Mifflin and Co., 1942.
_____. *On Becoming a Person*. Boston: Houghton, Mifflin and Co., 1961.
Wexler, David, and Rice, Laura, eds. *Innovations in Client-Centered Therapy*. New York: John Wiley and Sons, 1974.

5. TRANSPERSONAL THERAPY

Assagioli, Robert. *The Act of Will*. Baltimore: Penguin Books, 1974.
_____. *Psychosynthesis*. New York: Viking Press, 1971.
Haronian, Frank. "Psychosynthesis." *Journal of Humanistic Psychology* 15 (Fall 1975).

6. LOGOTHERAPY

Crumbaugh, James et al. *Logotherapy: New Help for Problem Drinkers*. Chicago: Nelson-Hall, 1980.
Frankl, Viktor. *The Doctor and the Soul: From Psychotherapy to Logotherapy*. New York: Vintage Books, 1973.
_____. *Man's Search for Meaning: Introduction to Logotherapy*. New York: Simon and Schuster, 1962.
_____. *Psychotherapy and Existentialism: Selected Papers on Logotherapy*. New York: Simon and Schuster, 1967.
_____. *The Will to Meaning*. New York: Simon and Schuster, 1962.
The International Forum for Logotherapy: Journal of the Search for Meaning.

F. FEMINIST THERAPY

Bardwick, Judith, ed. *Readings in Psychology of Women*. New York: Harper and Row, 1972.
Berlin, Sharon. "Better Work with Women Clients." *Social Work* 21:6 (November 1976).
Broverman, Inge et al. "Sex Role Stereotypes: A Current Appraisal." *Journal of Social Issues* 28 1972.

Chesler, Phyllis. *Women and Madness*. New York: Doubleday and Co., 1972.
Franks, Violet, and Burtle, Vasanti. *Women in Therapy: New Psychotherapies for a Changing Society*. New York: Brunner/Mazel, 1974.
Freeman, Jo, ed. *Women: A Feminist Perspective*. Palo Alto, Calif.: Mayfield Publishing Co., 1975.
Gornick, Vivian, and Moran, Barbara, eds. *Women in Sexist Society*. New York: Signet Books, 1972.
Johnson, Marilyn. "An Approach to Feminist Therapy." *Psychotherapy: Theory, Research and Practice* 13 (Spring 1976).
Klein, Marjorie. "Feminist Concepts of Therapy Outcome." *Psychotherapy: Theory, Research and Practice* 13 (Spring 1976).
Krakauer, Alice. "Woman's Body, Woman's Mind: A Good Therapist is Hard to Find." *Ms.* 1 (October 1972).
Mander, Anica, and Rush, Ann. *Feminism As Therapy*. New York: Random House, 1974.
Marecek, Jeanne, and Kravetz, Diane. "Women and Mental Health: A Review of Feminist Change Efforts." *Psychiatry* 40 (November 1977).
Miller, Jean, ed. *Psychoanalysis and Women*. New York: Brunner/Mazel, 1973.
Pincus, Cynthia; Radding N.; and Larence, R. "A Professional Counseling Service for Women." *Social Work* 19 (March 1974).
Rawlings, Edna, and Carter, Dianne, eds. *Psychotherapy for Women: Treatment Toward Equality*. Springfield, Ill.: Charles C Thomas, 1977.
Sanville, Jean, and Shor, Joel. "Women in Transcendence: Clinical Pathways to Change." *Clinical Social Work Journal* 3 (Spring 1975).
Stevens, Barbara. "The Psychotherapist and Women's Liberation." *Social Work* 16 (July 1971). Also in *Differential Diagnosis and Treatment in Social Work*. Edited by Francis Turner. New York: The Free Press, 1968, 2d ed., 1976.
Wesley, Carol. "The Women's Movement and Psychotherapy." *Social Work* 21 (March 1975).
Williams, Elizabeth. *Notes of a Feminist Therapist*. New York: Dell Publishing Co., 1977.
Wortis, Helen, and Rabinowitz, Clara, eds. *The Women's Movement: Social and Psychological Perspectives—American Orthopsychiatric Association*. New York: Halsted Press, 1972.

VI. Evolving Casework Practice: Approaches and Issues

Alexander, Leslie. "Social Work's Freudian Deluge: Myth or Reality." *Social Service Review* 46 (December 1972).

Ambrosino, Salvatore. "Integrating Counseling, Family Life Education, and Family Advocacy." *Social Casework* 60 (December 1979).

Bakalinsky, Rosalie. "People vs. Profits: Social Work in Industry." *Social Work* 25 (November 1980).

Bernstein, Barton. "Malpractice: Future Shock of the 1980s." *Social Casework* 62 (March 1981).

_____. "The Social Worker as an Expert Witness." *Social Casework* 58 (July 1977).

Blomquist, David; Gray, Daniel; and Smith, Larry. "Social Work in Business and Industry." *Social Casework* 60 (October 1979).

Borkman, Thomasina. "Experiential Knowledge: A New Concept for the Analysis of Self-Help Groups." *Social Service Review* 50 (September 1976).

Boyd, Lawrence, Jr.; Hylton, John; and Price, Steven. "Computers in Social Work Practice: A Review." *Social Work* 23 (September 1978).

Briar, Scott. "The Future of Social Work: An Introduction." *Social Work* 19 (September 1974).

Brooks, Paul. "Industry-Agency Program for Employee Counseling." *Social Casework* 56 (July 1975).

Cantoni, Lucile. "Family Life Education: A Treatment Modality." *Child Welfare* 54 (November 1975).

Daley, Michael. "Burnout: Smoldering Problem in Protective Services." *Social Work* 24 (September 1979).

Edelwick, Jerry, and Brodsky, Archie. *Burnout: Stages of Disillusionment in the Helping Professions*. New York: Human Sciences Press, 1980.

Ewalt, Patricia, and Cohen, Margrit. "Total Agency Issues and the Short-term Grant." *Social Casework* 56 (June 1975).

Fischer, Joel. "Is Casework Effective?" *Social Work* 18 (January 1973).

Frailberg, Selma. "Psychoanalysis and Social Work: A Re-Examination of the Issues." *Smith College Studies in Social Work* 48 (March 1978).

Green, Ronald, and Cox, Gibbi. "Social Work and Malpractice: A Converging Course." *Social Work* 23 (March 1978).

Hallowitz, David. "Advocacy in the Context of Treatment." *Social Casework* 55 (July 1974).

Harrison, W. David. "Role Strain and Burnout in Child Protective Services Workers." *Social Service Review* 54 (March 1980).

Katz, Alfred, and Bender, Eugene. *The Strength in Us: Self-Help Groups in the Modern World*. New York: New Viewpoints, 1976.

Keefe, Thomas. "Meditation and the Psychotherapist." *American Journal of Orthopsychiatry* 45 (April 1975).

Kurzman, Paul. "Private Practice as a Social Work Function." *Social Work* 21 (September 1976).

Levick, Keith. "Privileged Communication: Does It Really Exist?" *Social Casework* 62 (April 1981).

Levin, Arnold. "Private Practice Is Alive and Well." *Social Work* 2 (September 1976).

Levine, Richard. "Socal Worker Malpractice." *Social Casework* 57 (July 1976).

Levy, Charles. "Inputs versus Outputs as Criteria of Competence." *Social Casework* 55 (June 1974).

"Looking Forward: Social Work in the Eighties." *Social Work*. Entire issue. 19 (September 1974).

McGowan, Brenda. "The Case Advocacy Function in Child Welfare Practice." *Child Welfare* 57 (May 1978).

MacLoughlin, Anna, and Pinkus, Helen. "The Role of a Clinical Social Worker in a Changing Society." *Journal of Education for Social Work* 10 (Spring 1974).

Mantell, Joanne; Alexander, Esther; and Kleiman, Mark. "Social Work and Self-Help Groups." *Health and Social Work* 1 (February 1976).

Meyer, Carol. "What Directions for Direct Practice." *Social Work* 24 (July 1979).

Nelson, Ronald, and Kelly, Kathleen. "Audit Review: Requirement or Significant Help?" *Child Welfare* 59 (May 1980).

Ozawa, Martha. "Development of Social Services in Industry: Why and How?" *Social Work* 25 (November 1980).

Panitch, Arnold. "Advocacy in Practice." *Social Work* 19 (May 1974).

Perlman, Helen. "Confessions, Concerns and Commitment of an Ex-Clinical Social Worker." *Clinical Social Work Journal* 2 (Fall 1974).

Pharis, Mary. "Paraprofessionals in Clinical Social Work: Do They Belong?" *Clinical Social Work Journal* (Fall 1973).

Prochaska, Janice, and Fallon, Beth. "Preparing a Community for Family Life Education." *Child Welfare* 58 (December 1979).

Reynolds, Mildred. "Privacy and Privilege: Patients; Professionals' and the Public's Rights." *Clinical Social Work Journal* 5 (Spring 1977).

————. "Threats to Confidentiality." *Social Work* 21 (March 1976).

Rosenberg, Marvin, and Brody, Ralph. "The Threat or Challenge of Accountability." *Social Work* 19 (May 1974).

Sands, Rosalind, and Young, Arthur. "The Retooling of a Child Guidance Center: Changes and Changeover for the Tasks of the Seventies." *American Journal of Orthopsychiatry.* 43 (January 1973).

Schodek, Kay. "Adjuncts to Social Casework in the 1980s." *Social Casework* 62 (April 1981).

Schoech, Dick, and Schkade, Lawrence. "Computers Helping Caseworkers' Decision Support Systems." *Child Welfare* 59 (November 1980).

Schroeder, Leila. "Legal Liability: A Professional Concern." *Clinical Social Work Journal* 7 (Fall 1979).

Senna, Joseph. "Changes in Due Process of Law." *Social Work* 19 (May 1974).

Simon, Dawn. "A Systematic Approach to Family Life Education." *Social Casework* 57 (October 1976).

Simons, Ronald, and Aigner, Stephen. "Facilitating an Eclectic Use of Practice Theory." *Social Casework* 60 (April 1979).

Stanley, Joe. "Experiences Based Guidelines for the Future of Direct Services." *Smith College Studies in Social Work* 43 (February 1973).

Stromer, Walter. "Feedback for Helpers." *Social Work* 20 (May 1975).

Suarez, Mary, and Ricketson, Mary. "Facilitating Casework with Protective Service Clients Through Use of Volunteers." *Child Welfare* 53 (May 1974).

Wald, Esther. *The Remarried Family: Challenge and Promise.* New York: Family Service Association of America, 1981.

Weiss, David. "A Humanistic Design for Practice." *Social Casework* 55 (March 1974).

NOTES

NOTES

OF RELATED INTEREST

Forgive Me No Longer:
The Liberation of Martha

ESTHER FIBUSH and MARTHA MORGAN

A compelling and unique success story written by a therapist and her client shows how therapeutic understanding develops on both sides of the desk.

Ideal as a teaching text

The student can learn what occurs during therapy:

▶ Transcribed records of crucial therapeutic work during each session provide an extraordinary sense of immediacy and intimacy.

▶ Notebooks kept by both women provide additional insight into more "unconscious" or nonverbal aspects of the therapeutic process.

▶ Professional and personal reactions are intertwined to show what actually happens as the therapy progresses.

Illustrates how to deal with an old set of problems in a new way and how change, growth, and self-realization are achieved by both therapist and client.

"...an instructive text for students and experienced practitioners of psychotherapy...a remarkable book."
— Carel B. Germain, D.S.W., Columbia University and University of Connecticut

Interviewing: Its Principles and Methods

ANNETTE GARRETT

Third edition revised and enlarged by
MARGARET M. MANGOLD and ELINOR P. ZAKI

A complete study of how to plan and conduct interviews successfully.

The international classic that has been translated into nineteen foreign languages — and is also available in Braille and on phonograph records.

▶ A must for social work students!
▶ An ideal gift for any professional who deals with people. (Used and referred to so extensively that many social workers are on their third and fourth copies.)

The basic text for teaching interviewing to social workers, nurses, teachers, physicians, psychologists, community activity volunteers, and personnel in industry and government.

Strength to Families

**FAMILY SERVICE
ASSOCIATION
OF AMERICA**
44 East 23rd Street
New York, N.Y. 100

ISBN 0-87304-193